ECHOES OF THUNDER

A Unique Experience in Reincarnation

by **Harry L. Green**

EMERALD HOUSE
P.O. Box 1769
Sandpoint, Idaho 83864
208-263-1071

Published by
████████████
████████
████████████

Copyright 1980
ISBN #0-936958-00-6, hard cover
ISBN #0-936958-01-4, paperback
Library of Congress Catalog #80-66322

Cover design by Luna Moth

ACKNOWLEDGMENT

This book was written during the winter of 1972-73. When it was presented to the editors of several large publishing houses, they suggested re-writes and offered analyses, up-dated market information and encouragement. But they didn't want to publish this book. Stories on reincarnation weren't that popular just then. This wasn't deflating but it brought us to heel, as it were.

An acknowledgment is appropriate to explain the "we/us". It is not the time-encrusted editorial 'we' which I have always looked on as an affectation. WE are foremost Carol and Harry, what we believe to be a rare coming together of twin souls in a mortal incarnation. WE are also the Poet whose patience and guidance from another level of consciousness gave life to these words before they appeared on paper. WE are Keetoowah, one of our soulmates. WE are all the entities, in whatever form, who contributed to the effort we now offer to you.

Tiresome obstacles arose, illness, family problems, what-have-you. Then we reached for the fine-tuning knob and got the message. This work could not be published until we had again come together with another part of our eternal family unit, one of our soulmates. An entity who has been literally a part of us as long as individual consciousness has existed. And always will be. This entity is Keetoowah, who chose to enter this fragment of eternity as a member of the Cherokee Nation a little over 60 years ago.

Keetoowah knew we were coming to join him in Northern California where we now live. He became grumpier and more impatient for a year and a half until we arrived. We don't know the scope of Keetoowah's awareness except as he reveals it to us. We do know he was an integral part of many of the past lives we have recorded and that he has total recall of every earth lifetime we have shared.

Whatever we are in the cosmic scheme of things, Keetoowah belongs. He is now friend, mentor, invaluable source of information and, if I can ever teach him to read a road map he will be our revered and respected Faithful Indian Guide. In all fairness, I must admit we reach destinations more readily when he rides beside the driver and points a finger saying, "That way" when we come to an intersection. I still wish he could read a road map.

The beloved old coot may have delayed publication of this book for seven years until he could growl his way through the manuscript but he didn't challenge anything. He remembers what we remember, and we needed the blending of these memories to bring this work to completion. It is this happy reunion that has given added joy and fullness to the pages that follow. It's just as well. It's a heavy thing to argue semantics with an Indian, especially when he has a PhD.

I

The girl sat on the floor, across the coffee table from me. An OUIJA board lay between us. I explained, as I always do with strangers, "We are using the board because this is the first time we have met. This is a gadget familiar to all of us, and in this way we can all participate. OK?"

The four other people nodded and I spoke directly to the entity whose presence had brought us together. "You have been manifesting yourself visibly to your daughter here. This has frightened her and if you continue it could be physically dangerous to her. Do you know this?" The answer was slow in coming and I sensed stubbornness and antagonism. - I've been worried about her. - "You're not helping her, though, by frightening her." - I don't want to frighten her. I just want her to know I still care about her. - And so it went, an earth-bound spirit trying in a futile, stumbling way to mitigate his guilt at having passed over leaving only debts and hardship for a widow and five children.

I paused and spoke to them all, the man's widow, the teenager facing me, another daughter and her husband. "Your dead husband and father is bound not only by his own guilt. He feels he has wronged you, but so do you. Your resentment is also holding him. I want you now to turn your thoughts to love, and to the presence of God as the embodiment of love. I want you to find it in your hearts to forgive him." I asked them, individually, to forgive this tormented man. Individually, with tears in their eyes, they did It was a moment of drama, intensified by the anguish of the waiting man, the man who had left his body eight years before.

I spoke to him again, gently because it was now time. I called him by name, "I have a friend where you are, a friend who will go with you and guide you into the world where you should be. Do you want to go?" - Yes - "Very well." I turned my thoughts to a highly valued spirit friend known to me only as Pa. "Pa, will you take this entity, go with him, help him?" And he was gone, instantly. We all knew it. We were all glad. Now we could relax, laugh, have a few glasses of wine and get to know each other. I felt good because I had almost refused to see them. It could have been just another Sunday afternoon with nothing more constructive done than a day of watching professional football on TV.

Following a phoned introduction, a woman had called, explaining that her teenage daughter was being disturbed by repeated apparitions of the child's dead father. I was recovering from a serious illness and had no enthusiasm for a further energy drain, but this was a genuine call for help. It doesn't take a great nobility of character for one to permit his mind and spirit to be used as a vehicle through which to focus external powers and influences. Regrettably, many psychically endowed people use their powers to seek financial gain or as a means of launching themselves on a spiritually damaging ego trip. The exercise of these powers, however, is sometimes a strain on the body because the body is the channel through which flows an often turbulent and always unpredictable gamut of emotions. This knowledge caused my reluctance. I didn't want to put myself through another wringer when I was already exhausted. The overcoming of this hesitation marked the beginning of the most exciting period of a lifetime which had been by no means dull. It marked the reunion with the other half of me, with the woman who is now my wife.

And so I resumed my relationship with the one I believe is my soul twin, 20th Century widow, mother of five, from whom I had been separated for over fifty years. We shared an unsuccessful life together prior to this one, a life which ended in physical death for both of us in 1917.

Then as now, I have no inclination toward mediumship, even as a time-consuming sideline. I had been aware for most of my life that I was a psychic sensitive of some sort. I had a precognitive ability which enabled me to tune in on disasters such as earthquakes, humanity out of harmony as in riots, and the wrenching calamities of airplane crashes. . . before they happened. These glimpses of the immediate future were confided to a few friends and, almost without exception, proved accurate. I disciplined myself to tune these things out. My foreknowledge could be put to no use and the experiences frightened me. I was frightened because I was THERE, albeit briefly. I felt the grinding, shifting earth under my feet, trees lashing themselves to splinters, buildings crumbling and falling to crush terrorized masses of people. I shared terror before the implacable, invincible forces of a tidal wave and midst the berserk rage of howling mobs. I knew the moments of silence as the roar of a jetliner ceased and then shared in the screaming as it fell with monstrous slow-motion heaviness to smash itself to fragments against the earth. I saw, felt, and was afraid.

On the other hand, using this extra sense occasionally brought a joy which is experienced by too few who stumble along immersed in their own preoccupation with themselves and the unreality of the here and now. In a way I do not understand, I can sometimes alleviate physical pain by exerting slight pressure with fingers and hands on various parts of a sufferer's body, usually right behind the ears or directly on the affected area, perhaps over a broken bone or near a severely burned area. This is a gift for which I am supremely grateful because I am intimately familiar with physical pain, and have been for thirty years. I wish I could do these things better and reach more people.

The summation of my psychic sensitivities (I have an irrational dislike for the term "medium" as applied to myself) is that I regard them as mediocre at very best. I am regularly guided to people in trouble, as they are led to me, and as my body and senses can be used as a kind of spiritual transformer to focus helpful fragments of the Infinite onto and into them, I will do so. It is for only a few of these reasons, however, that I find myself in this particular lifetime.

The thrill of meeting one's completed self in the fullness of spiritual awareness beggars description. It is a far deeper thing than the stale-phrased "falling in love" and at nearly 50, we had both experienced what we thought was "love" several times. Meeting and knowing completion is the recognition of resuming a love which has endured throughout a span of eternity beyond man's imagination. It is an aching joy of fulfillment. It is also bawdy, raucous and downright fun. It is excited anticipation and a sober searching for a means to bring the objects of our hard-earned lessons and a measure of spiritual serenity to others.

Soon under the same roof and sharing the same last name, Carol and I begun to compare what we knew of the spiritual and psychic as we fitted our own lives from this earth experience into the communal pattern. She wondered why she had responded so immediately to the spiritual upon her first exposure to it a few years previously. I was more interested in the chemistry which had ignited our fire to each other so spontaneously. Recognition was virtually immediate and the wonder grew as we discovered improbable similarities in tastes and attitudes.

The two lives, hers and mine, emerged in a delightful, purposeful way which would stretch the probability of coincidence to the point of incredulity. We were born and grew to young maturity in adjoining states, never far apart... Kentucky and Virginia. At various times she lived in San Francisco (I lived two blocks away on the same street), she lived in Oregon (I was in Oregon), later she was in the city of Trier in Germany (so was I, at the same time), she had planned to end a several years' European odyssey in Greece but cancelled it when family emergencies arose (I was scheduled to go to Greece at the same time but cancelled it... because of family emergencies). There are more incidents when we were in the same place at the same time; yet, prior to February 1972, we had never met.

Carol shortly mastered the knack of spirit communication and we spent refreshing hours as I introduced her to friends now in spirit and reinforced her beliefs with evidential information from her early life which she had forgotten. I gently encouraged Carol to practice communication without the OUIJA board. The board is a crutch, it is not necessary and can be dreadfully dangerous if unwisely used. I used it during my early days with

Carol simply to speed up our communications; I concentrated on the board to recognize and eliminate interference. The results would have been the same if I had placed an unvarnished piece of pine plank on my lap.

Carol is an experienced, dedicated and hard working registered nurse. She gives much more than professionalism demands. She gives of herself. She gives love. This is a rare and wonderful gift for one who must deal daily with human misery and for this I shall always have for her a profound and even humble respect. Minor trouble arose but never surfaced over this. She frequently, during the day, gave all she had and there was little left for me at the end of the day. I tried very hard not to resent this, but I did.

By a similar token, she had had little to prepare her for life with a professional writer. This particular profession has been romanticized out of all proportion. Writers are just people who suffer from indigestion, worry about mortgage payments, raise families and often voice the wish that they had elected a career as a Maytag washing machine repairman. But writing is what they do for a living.

The sifting, sorting and melding of our lives was accomplished with high good humor. We chuckled, while admittedly challenging each other, over the sage misgivings of a number of friends who shook their heads and allowed as to how our relationship wouldn't last the summer out. We didn't have time to concern ourselves with much else than begin to wonder, now that we've got it, what do we do with it. We entertained, getting to know each other's friends and squishing me into her family life (all her kids then lived in the same town with us). We established a practice of daily Bible reading and began attending church regularly again. This wasn't startling behavior for a pair of reasonably respectable people but to us it was a thrill because we were doing it together.

Twin souls don't have the incredible, sparkling joy of re-meeting at an advanced stage of maturity just for the purpose of enjoying each other, though. Lovely as it was, our pleasure in each other was not the end-all. How then, to find the reason for our reunion and more important, what to do about it? We are fortunate in our lifetimes to be on what we feel is the neap tide of an opening spiritual awareness. We find ourselves in an age where we need not hide our candle neath a chamber pot, or however the expression goes.

The most gratifying responses were from countless people who were just as vitally interested in the realm of the spiritual as we were, but perhaps not as well informed. In a word, we found ourselves a part of a growing segment of society which was emerging from improbable cracks in the walls of traditional, institutionalized religionism. 'Religionism', as far as I know, is my own word. I like it.

We find more open minds within established denominations than one would expect. These are spiritually troubled times and many are seeking further reassurance than traditional dogma offers, yet do not know where to turn. People with a lifetime of Christianity behind them are unwilling to depart from the comfortable community of their familiar church, even though haunted with a growing conviction that they are being sold short within the framework of that church. It is very moving to see such a person expand with the wonder of realizing that there is nothing in the prayerful study of the psychic which is incompatible with the fundamental tenets of any religion.

The basic search of each mortal soul is for some encouragement that he will continue to exist. Carol and I had sought this affirmation individually and had found it long before meeting each other. We had also discovered the only true way of making it a fulfilling, emotionally satisfying thing. . . by according it the reverence of a religious experience. To us, religion doesn't connote long faces and somber rituals, even though with Protestant backgrounds we have found deep contentment in the dignified pageantry of a Catholic mass. But, what could be more joyful than the absolute knowledge that we are now but in a single phase of a life without end?

We share a largely unspoken agreement with most others of our persuasion in that we don't proselytize. We don't aim to win converts, but to help show the way for those who are spiritually ready, and we find many. The spirit is already at work within them; it only needs direction.

The foregoing is a capsule version of the countless hours of discussion we shared in the beginning of our lives together. One theme kept returning to us as our personal, strongest manifestation of eternal life. . . reincarnation. To me, there was no question that I had lived many lifetimes. I carried with me the detailed memory of one lived in Coventry, England in the late seventeenth century. Fragments of others were available by placing myself into a light, self-induced hypnotic trance. I am a fairly accomplished hypnotist although I have only used it with great caution. At her request, I tried to use hypnosis with Carol to release her consciousness enough to capture a few past lifetime memories of her own. Failing this, I attempted to show her the way to self hypnosis by losing herself in the living flame of a candle. Neither worked She isn't a good hypnotic subject.

We attained initial success when I introduced her to guided meditation. This informal rite is most rewarding when used with groups so the participants can compare experiences at its conclusion, but it is also effective on an individual basis. It consists of techniques similar to hypnosis except that the suggestion is repeatedly made to remember! The leader creates a verbal picture of the most relaxing surroundings he can muster.

My own favorite begins on a shaded country lane, followed by a leisurely stroll into a pine forest and finally a gliding boat ride across a peaceful lake to a lovely and secluded island. At each step I invoke all the senses one would use if actually there. . . the warmth of sunlight on the skin, the resilient feel of the earth underfoot, the smell of the pine trees, the sound of the wind whishing gently through them, the cool feel of the water and the serenity of the sanctuary as we reach the island. The ever-constant remember! is to fix every image and sensation so that it can be recalled at will. On my private island is a small stream which issues from a large cave. We enter this cave with much ceremony, feeling the refreshing coolness, and proceed to a softly lighted room.

We know by now that someone is awaiting us in that room, and it is here that I break off my narration and leave others to whatever spiritual entity they may meet there. Quite often nothing happens at all, and I have made the trip many times. Just as often, however, someone is there and messages of import are received. Whatever the end results, it's an extremely pleasant way to spend an hour.

Carol did well with this and it was but a step to controlled individual meditation. In the elementary stage of meditation one simply brings the mind to complete rest by systematically excluding all outer distractions. At this stage, and we did it together, images begin to flash on the blanked-out screen of our consciousness. She saw herself in different but recognizable bodies, she saw me, we saw us. These images which come with beginning meditation are common; their appearance simultaneously to two people is unusual and gave us our first clue that we had shared more than just a few lifetimes together. There was a tangible bond there, firm, strong and happy-making.

The decision to begin a chronicle of our own past lives was not made because we considered them worthy of immortalizing, but simply because we had access to them. To describe them, it was necessary to re-live them and to do that we needed help. This help came after a round robin of conferences with spirit friends not unlike editorial meetings while preparing a magazine article or a think tank session while working on an important advertising account. Within a week an entity emerged and introduced himself to us as the Poet. All we knew then of the Poet is that his last lifetime was spent as a Southern schoolteacher about the 1930's and 40's, and that he was a pipe smoker. We were chatting to unwind after a particularly tiring session one night and he commented on the pipe tobacco I used. I idly asked him what brand he used and the room was suddenly redolent with an aromatic smell of pipe tobacco, totally unlike my own brand. It is to the Poet to whom we are indebted for crystalizing our memories of past lives into a form which lent itself to coherent narration.

The true adventure of exploring your own segment of eternity lies in the fact that you never know what is coming next. The excitement is heightened as realization grows that the unfolding of lives is a very personal thing. . . all this actually happened to you at some moment in antiquity. One event stands stark and clear and at first glance appears to have been an alteration in the climax of a centuries-old happening. To us, it was unique; we have not read or heard of anything similar.

I do not recall the circumstances leading to this event although it was probably late evening, near the time when we went through our ritual meditation-Bible-reading-prayer-service. We were sitting quietly in bed with only a reading light on and I felt myself drifting into a trance. I have been in trance many times but had not tried it very often for several years. Tape recordings of my trance "sittings" revealed nothing very important and I remembered little of what went on. This evening I went willingly, however, in answer to an ancient, despairing cry of loneliness. The tape recorder was not convenient so Carol made a complete set of notes. Since my own memory will be forever incomplete, I have asked her to transcribe her notes.

I knew, immediately, that he was going into trance although I had only seen him in trance a few times before. His eyes took on a far away expression of seeing beyond his present environment, and his breathing became very shallow. I took a pad and pencil and waited. He had told me repeatedly to note what he said in case he went into a trance because his memory of what he said in trance was never clear.

His eyes closed and several minutes passed with the only sound an incoherent mumbling. I was afraid the experience would be lost, but suddenly his voice became clear.

"Bete'ka," he whispered softly. "Small. . . dark. . . lonely and afraid. . ." His voice became louder. "You went there alone but you won't have to do it again because I will go back with you." He paused. "I will take your hand," he said reassuringly. "It is very cold, and when one is lonely and cold, that is very bad." His voice had a bleak and desolate sound. He repeated, "I will go back with you and hold your hand. I'll put my arm around you and go with you. You will be warm when we die. You will not have to die alone. . ."

His face suddenly contorted with an expression of grief. "Poor little frightened thing!" He began to sob with harsh, choking sounds. Tears ran down his cheeks. "No!" he pleaded. "Don't be frightened. I've been with you so long. Didn't you know that? Haven't you figured it out?"

There was another pause while his face relaxed and he consoled, softly. "See? It's almost over. You aren't cold and you don't hurt." Suddenly his voice sharpened. "No! Don't look back. No!"

"No, I know you have to go that way. . . that's all right. I'll be back. Now there's much more beyond the hunter's heart. Go on. . . no, you'll not be lost." He paused as if listening, then cautioned, "But don't do it too soon just because it looks so beautiful. You don't know that world yet. Don't be afraid. . .

*not like that". His voice grew wistful, tender, "Anas, anika. . ."
and faded away.*

*I became aware of my surroundings again, and of Carol snuffling into
a tissue. I knew something important had occurred and before it could
elude me, I told her, "You were young, inexperienced, possessed of the
streak of wildness which has always marked you. You were a member of a
tribe of people, possibly Indians. You became pregnant by a man who was
already mated to another woman. The penalty was irrevocable. You were
sent into the wastelands without provisions, to die."*

*We have not succeeded in filling in the missing parts of this incident. It
is still much like the transcript of one-half of a telephone conversation, but
we treasure it because of the powerful emotional content it still holds for
us. The fascinating aspect, initially, was that I had apparently returned to
the past and altered it. Subsequent investigation has shown that this is not
quite the way it was. I had only succeeded in altering her memory of this
fragment of the past. . . This research would be impossible without the aid
of our spirit friends, notably the Poet who is editor, critic, friend.*

*As it was finally assembled, the story was that Carol, as the wayward
Indian maid, still retained in some area of her memory the terror of a
lonely death, probably from exposure, which had haunted her for centuries.
This memory apparently came near enough to the surface for some part
of my consciousness to grasp and respond to it. In a trance state, I was
able to overcome temporal limitations of space and time, enter this
remote area of her memory and re-create the terrifying experience of her
lonely and shameful death. I superimposed myself onto this memory,
joining her in it by virtue of the fact that we have been united since time
began. Now, when that part of her consciousness harks back to that time,
the memory is of having gone through it with me, her comforter, her mate.*

*One of our earliest shared memories of an earlier lifetime took us
back several hundred years to the vastness of the North American West.
Late one night we were riffling through the files, so to speak, and a visual
image appeared which we were able to lock onto. We saw it at the same
time, a young, lissome Indian woman walking away from us. She carried
something on her shoulder, possibly a pottery jug of water. Her hair, jet
black, streamed in cascades down her back almost to her waist. Utterly
charmed, we watched and then Carol caught her breath. "That's me!" It
was indeed and we knew immediately I was there, too, and could see her,
although my image never appeared.*

*The revelation was transitory, not more than five minutes, but in that
time Carol knew she clutched some garment to partially cover her face.
The summer wind was blowing fiercely and sand stung her skin. She felt
the smooth movement of muscles in her body, the grace and ease with
which she moved. She felt the dry heat of a summer of long ago. As the
sensory perceptions were heightened, memories of this other life began to*

flow. These memories were fragmented, though, and it was left to the Poet to fit them into chronological order and guide us gently along the paths we had trod together in one of the richest, fullest lives we have yet explored.

Perhaps the most critical facet in our selection of which lifetimes to chronicle was our affinity for that particular lifetime. In the recounting of the lives we spent as American Indians we were reminded again and again of a years-long feeling of closeness to the Indian of the American southwest. We responded with love to their art, their history of impregnable dignity which still survives but, most of all, to the people themselves. We were drawn to them and they responded to us as they did to few white people. While nursing Indian children in New Mexico, Carol was often mistaken for Indian by a child's parents. . . to which she responded with thanks but had to say she was sorry but she didn't speak Navajo, Zuni or Apache.

We visited pueblos and ruins and even retraced the probable path of the wandering tribes. We learned to read the petroglyphs, the relief carvings left by the roving clans. We found centuries-old histories of up to four migrations in Colorado, Northern New Mexico and over a thousand miles into the interior of Old Mexico.

And so it was with love in our hearts that we opened our memories to live again in the harsh, still untamed beauty of what is now part of the state of Arizona. As these memories assumed form, the great vault of eternity opened, the mists of time that always is cleared like a summer storm and we responded to the echoes of its thunder.

II

The wind blew free in the land of the Mesa people. It tore across the high mesas in summer, dropping sand and pebbles into the water stored in stone cisterns atop the houses, it drew the hot ashes out of the cooking fires onto the bare feet of the women, causing them to dance and utter dark imprecations against the capricious sky gods. The wind brought the heavy snows of winter but instead of letting them rest, whipped them into monstrous contoured drifts flanked by stone-frozen bare ground. The wind washed the night skies and let the stars blaze fiercely and unwinking through a crystal atmosphere. The wind told the old ones of the subtle changes of the seasons; it challenged the young ones to race it and fill themselves with this brief moment of eternity.

The women spoke wonderingly of the great wind which blew when the girl was born. Seemingly infected by this force, the child showed such a supernormal activity her mother and grandmother called her the Lively Wonder. By the time she was four, the child's name had been altered to Wild Witch by her family, who repeated the windstorm story of her birth night so often the child thought she remembered it herself. It was the Wild Witch in the youngster who tethered the ponies of the hunters to the legs of their tepees when they were camped in the fields, then set the horses to galloping. She also contrived a woven latticework which, when properly positioned, caught the wind and vibrated with a fearful moan. She concealed this device near the ceremonial dancing place and serious debate arose urging the moving of the site elsewhere. A playmate discovered the device, however, and demonstrated it to the embarrassed tribal elders.

This playmate exposed her because he realized more than she the seriousness which would be involved in the consecrating of a new ceremonial ground. He was filled with the vitality of life himself and was occasionally her accomplice when her planned escapades sufficiently fired his imagination. He was different, she knew, and he frequently drove her to frenzy with his long silences and strange eyes, but she was never completely happy unless near him. He was born shortly after the Wild One, in the somnolence of a springtime afternoon, so easily that his young mother forced insincere shrieks from her throat to impress the assembled older women. A happy and undemanding baby, he was adored and pampered by the women who cooed when he smiled at them and called him their little White Mouse. His mother intended to consult with the elders to seek an omen which would give him a more fitting name but never got around to it, so it was as White Mouse that the most beloved sage of his generation lived and died.

The men of the tribe attached no importance to male children until they were ready for their warrior's initiation. The birth of a boy was usually celebrated with an impromptu all-night dance begun by the father if he and his friends weren't busy with hunting or fishing. When not preoccupied with their own nostalgia, the old men occasionally showed the boy-children how to make weapons and recited long-winded accounts of their own former prowess as hunters. Mostly, boy-children were left to be children until they became man-size and, therefore, useful.

The tribe in general paid no attention at all to female children so Wild Witch and White Mouse grew to adolescence sharing the wisdom they gained from bright-eyed observation of the world around them and silent communion with the all-protective Great One whom they recognized as being a part of themselves. They were ordered into the fields in season to tend the grain but a sharp eye could have spotted them high up a terrifying cliff where they crouched motionless for hours watching a mother eagle bring food to its brood. One chore they did not shirk was the onerous task of carrying water from the river up to the mesa top in the dry seasons. They knew well the precious value of water.

White Mouse dogged sturdily after the adult hunters and by observation and practice refined his hunting skills while other boys his age played at war games and occasionally shot each other with their makeshift arrows. His graceful stealth, patience and skill won the attention and grudging admiration of the mature hunters and he was accorded the great honor of being invited to join them when he was twelve. White Mouse hunted alone, though. With infinite patience, he would separate an antelope from its brothers, then pace it with his pony across the plains until it fell exhausted and despairing to its knees. Before killing it, he would solemnly intone, "I regret that you must give your life to fill the bellies of my people. I respect your soul, which will survive you."

Wild Witch could not ride with him because the men would never entrust a precious pony to a girl-child. The ponies would seldom breed when tamed; the capturing and breaking of them consumed many exhausting days. Wild Witch singled her own pony out in a wild herd, stalked it into a rock crevice and subdued it during a day and a night of wild shrieks and threats. Now able to ride with him, Wild Witch laughed at him the first time she witnessed this ritual of slaying. "Why do you apologize to an animal when you must kill it? Is it not the Great One's scheme of things to provide the animals and fish that we may live?"

He was silent for so long she thought he was not going to reply. "I do not know the Great One's scheme of things. I only know that this creature had life, even as I do. I also know I have lived before and shall live forever."

"But what about the animal?" she said. "Is the same true for it?"

"That I cannot tell you because I do not know." He smiled. "What harm, though, to give the poor creature a few words of reassurance?"

She was not satisfied. "But how do you always KNOW things? You have not learned it from our elders because this is not their teaching."

He looked up from his work on the dead animal. "I remember."

"But how can you remember things which have never happened to you?"

He looked across the plain and frowned, the expression giving an ageless maturity to his young face which made her quiet. "I don't know," he said. "And sometimes it disturbs me."

"Do you remember everything?"

"Yes."

"Do you even remember being born?"

"Yes, I remember that. I was cradled long in a warm and comfortable fluid. Then the fluid was gone and I was dry. I forced myself out into loud sounds and terrible daylight. It is a frightening thing, being born."

She sat facing him in the grass, her hands folded in her lap. "If it's so bad, can you remember why you were born?"

"I'm not sure. I think it was because I wanted to be."

She stood. "Well, if we don't get this meat back before dark, you'll wish you never had been born. Let me help you."

It was not until the summer of his eighteenth year that White Mouse underwent the stressful initiation admitting him to the world of men. He had been scheduled for this rite the previous year but had quietly and reasonably argued with the Warrior-Chief that warrior training was a waste. After all, there had been no war within the memory of the Mesa people. They lived in a state of uneasy truce with the nomadic and sometimes marauding Dine. There was history of skirmishes with the Apaches far to the South and West but only when their hunting parties invaded the hunting territories of the Apaches in years of scarcity. The Warrior-Chief was a formidable man of great strength but blessed with tolerance and humor. So he deferred to the young man rather than search for arguments which had no logical basis. He was a knowledgable man, willing to let the passage of another year temper the young White Mouse's reasoning and obvious intelligence.

At initiation time the following year White Mouse took his place among those who announced themselves ready to take on the responsibilities of manhood. He was dark from the sun, lean and corded with muscle which seemed to draw his skin tight to the flesh.

Following six days of games and tests of stamina, the initiates lay prostrate and sweating, awaiting the moment of sunset which signified the end of the ordeal. The Warrior-Chief stepped to White Mouse and prodded him good-naturedly in the rump with the butt end of his spear. "Stand up, White-Mouse-who-has-become-Charging-Buffalo."

White Mouse stood and, on this signal, the others stood with him, wiping the sweat and dust from their bodies with their hands. "What has happened to our White Mouse?" the Warrior-Chief said, staggering White Mouse with an affectionate slap across the shoulders. "He swoops more swiftly than an eagle after a hare, his strength is that of ten lions. He has cracked the bones of three of my best warriors so badly they are unable to be here to witness his victory. Give the oration, White Mouse. You are the man of the hour."

The tribe drew closer and sat on the ground, hugging their knees and whispering to each other of past orations, both poor and splendid, which had been heard on these occasions. White Mouse waited for quiet and began to speak, his voice husky after his days of exertion. "This is not a happy time for me, my brothers. I did not make my warrior's mark at the appointed time because there was no war. Why, I asked myself, should I train myself in the ways of killing and maiming my fellow man when I know of no man who has done me hurt?"

"What would you have us do, White Mouse?" said a warrior he had bested in wrestling the day before. "Women's work?"

White Mouse stood smiling through the general laughter. "Is it women's work to build storehouses so our grain will not become wet from the rain and snow and spoil? Is it women's work to ride an extra day to where the game is more plentiful so we will have the juices of the summer-killed meat to feed our hunger when the snow is deep?"

There was grumbling from the men which was angrily shushed by those who recalled that it was White Mouse who, with a reluctant party of three or four hunters, had ridden the extra day many times and returned with meat which was dried and kept the hunger from many during the cold times. "This is not a warrior's oration," the Warrior-Chief chided. "It is a squabble fit only for women."

"I have become a warrior because I will soon be needed as a warrior," White Mouse said. "Even now an enemy approaches us from the West, his shadow bathed in the blood-red of the setting sun. He wears on his head a covering which catches and sends back the sunlight like the waves seen on the river at noon. He brings a weapon more terrible than the spear or arrow. He is dark of skin but not like we are and he carries the blackness of death within his breast."

The stillness of the people was profound. Every ear strained to hear the next words. When he also remained quiet, abashed at the effect he had caused, the Warrior-Chief stepped forward. "How do you know this, White Mouse?"

"It was all revealed to me in a dream."

"And you spoke of it to no person?"

"A man is not permitted to speak before the tribe before the ordeal. I have spoken of it to my woman, Lively Wonder, the one whom we call the Wild Witch."

There was murmuring throughout the assembly. Some shook their heads sadly over the folly of a younger generation which would reveal a message of such import to a mere woman. Others gravely approved White Mouse's rigid adherence to the Law. All were impressed, however, to see that the tribe again numbered among its midst one with the gift of prophecy. The gift would have to be tested, of course, and this would be difficult because the old seer had died many years ago.

"Is there more, White Mouse?" the Warrior-Chief said gently.

"Only that we must make our weapons ready. The enemy will be here before the first snow."

"But do you know beyond doubt that the stranger is our enemy?" the Warrior-Chief persisted.

"I am in error," White Mouse said, hanging his head. "In truth, I do not know the stranger is our enemy. I can only report that he imparted to me a feeling of anger and brutality."

"Prophecies can have many interpretations," the Warrior-Chief said. "Tomorrow you must meet with the tribal chief and the elders.

Tonight you will rest while the others do their orations and prepare for the dance."

The strangers were four days distant when word of their coming was brought by a runner from the tribe which lived on the mesa by the red hills. The messenger was questioned exhaustively and in detail and his description fitted White Mouse's oft-repeated version of them, even to the strange weapons they carried which could kill a deer or buffalo with a single blast. They were traveling slowly because they brought with them huge wheeled wagons drawn by strange animals which appeared to be large horses with long ears. The strangers did not appear to be threatening, the messenger said, but were greatly excited by the jewelry the old men in the tribe had fashioned from bits of silver and yellow metals. None of them could understand this. The metals were too soft to be fashioned into useful utensils and too heavy when made into kettles to be used for carrying water. Besides, there was very little to be found.

The elders waited with the chief when the strangers arrived and made camp at the base of their mesa by the river. They watched in silence as the strangers' envoy, a man of their own kind but oddly dressed in coarse woolen cloth and heavy leather boots, climbed the pathway to meet them. The man's speech was different but understandable and he made much of the fact that he could also speak in the language of the strangers. And what did the strangers want. . .? Only to rest in peace while they refreshed themselves and did a few days hunting. If the chief would send his best hunters, the strangers would share the fall of game from their dreadful sounding weapons.

Although he felt a coldness in his belly when near the strangers, White Mouse could find nothing unreasonable in the offer, so he led the party of hunters down to meet them. The strangers asked to be led to a buffalo herd, which the hunters did with reluctance. Although the buffalo offered the finest meat and skins, it was seldom hunted by them. An unpredictable, fearsome beast, it was extremely dangerous to hunt and was sought only when famine threatened from lack of other game. They held back as the strangers rode into the herd, shooting their loud weapons until six or seven giant buffalo lay dead within a few minutes.

When the huge carcasses were brought back to camp, they

were cut into sections rather than flayed into strips for drying in the sun. Big lumps of salt were taken from the wagons and shaved into powder with metal axes and knives. The salt was rubbed into the meat by the men who tended the wagons and did the cooking. This, explained the self-important interpreter, would preserve the meat. When it was ready for eating, one need only boil the salt away and cook it in the normal manner. The tribal chief then sent word for the women to descend from the mesa to learn the process.

White Mouse stood aside, watching the graceful women swinging their hips as they came down the path. Disturbed, he turned his attention to the strangers. Several were grouped together, laughing and poking each other in the ribs. White Mouse sensed that the strangers desired the women. He could understand how a man who was only with other men would want women but he failed to comprehend how men of honor could covet women belonging to someone else. Although it was not unusual for adolescent boys and girls to lie with each other, when the mating was accomplished it endured for life.

He hesitated about approaching the chief with his misgivings because no overt act had been committed. And the chief was busy, organizing all the men to ride to the salt lick a day to the South. The strangers agreed to send one of their wagons with a driver to bring back quantities of the salt which would more than preserve an entire winter's supply of meat.

Catching the excitement of the new venture, every man of age and even some of the old ones, rode to the salt lick burdened with cutting tools. They reached the area at first dark and camped to await the wagon which the strangers had assured would follow the next day.

White Mouse and Wild Witch lay apart on his blanket, moving together when the air cooled. She chuckled softly and he knew she was remembering the bafflement of the strangers when she, the lone female, had ridden out with the men. When the interpreter had explained, as he had been told, that it was to be expected because this was the tribe's Wild Witch, several of the strangers had made an odd crossing motion before their bodies with their hands.

White Mouse extended his arm and drew her head onto his shoulder. "You should have stayed with the women," he said. "The time is near for my sister and two others."

"The Old Mother is there," she said. "She was midwife for both you and me and I'm sure she still knows how."

"But the Old Mother does not have the gift," he said.

"I have no gift. I only do what I know best how to do. I am no good at making moccasins or weaving but I am good at bringing babies into the world alive."

They lay together long in the night, not sleeping, as they often did. They had learned in childhood how to refresh themselves in body and spirit with little sleep so they lay together this night, murmuring to each other when they saw an occasional meteor and when the earth wheeled them under the great constellations so they shifted their positions in the sky. She stroked his chest with her hand. "The day will come soon," she said. "And the work will be hard. Shall we sleep till then?"

"Yes," he said.

But he did not sleep, and she knew. "You are not sleeping." It was a question.

"No. I am listening."

"For what?"

"For the wagon of the strangers coming to help us with the salt. I do not hear it. It is not coming."

She knew that he listened with some part of his mind closed to her and not with his ears. She felt a coldness in her bones and sat up beside him, hugging herself. "I will awaken the chief," she said.

"I will get our horses," he said. "We must ride back at once."

The chief was annoyed at being awakened and adamantly refused to rouse the camp because of what he dismissed as the silly summer dream of a midwife. The Warrior-Chief awakened, however, and offered to ride with them. "I will ride half-way," he said. "If the wagon was driven through the night it will be more than half-way here. Then I can return and tell you."

The three spoke little as they rode into the daylight. White Mouse's face was drawn with anxiety and then pinched with anger as they reached the half-way point at mid morning. They dismounted to rest their ponies and White Mouse drew a diagram in the dust. "Wild Witch and I will go directly to the mesa. It will be shorter if we approach from the East." To the Warrior-Chief, "Return in all haste and bring the men. The strangers have betrayed us."

Not questioning his instant obedience to the crisp orders of an eighteen-year-old boy, the Warrior-Chief set off at full gallop in the direction they had come, his own heart now heavy with dread.

Topping a small hill, White Mouse and Wild Witch saw their mesa sharply outlined against the sky. He pointed and she nodded. There was no smoke rising in the still air from the always-burning cooking fires. They rode the few remaining miles until they had to leave their ponies at the foot of the mesa. "You go up," he said. "There are those there who are hurt and will need you. I will get another horse from the corral and go after them."

"You will go after them alone?" she said, her eyes wide.

He took her hands in his. "No, my Wild One, not alone. They

have left their vibrations of evil in the air which will be easier to follow than tracks in fresh snow." He extended an arm to the South and West. "They have gone back the way they came, probably passing near us in the night. I will intercept our people and we will have them by nightfall."

She shuddered, reluctant to start up the path. "Have they killed them all?"

He looked up, closing his eyes for a few moments. "You will find death there, but your first duty is to the living. We will return the rest of the women tomorrow to help prepare the dead for burial."

"You mean they took the women with them?"

"Yes. They plan to use them and keep them as slaves."

She tossed her head scornfully. "Our women will not let themselves be used as slaves. They will kill themselves first."

"I know. That is why I must hurry."

There was frenzied screaming when White Mouse met the men and told them what had happened. The Warrior-Chief quieted them with a roar. "We must use only the ears of White Mouse," he said. "And we must also abide by the wisdom the Great One has imparted to our new prophet. Tell us what to do, White Mouse."

"They do not know the land so they will follow the river," White Mouse said. "We will ride to the West and then South to where the river turns and await them when the night comes."

Led by White Mouse, the men were resting, concealed a mile from the river when the strangers' caravan stopped to make camp. They grunted with satisfaction as they saw the strangers posting guards at intervals along the route they had taken, leaving the Southern, down-river area of the camp exposed.

The Warrior-Chief numbed several heads with his huge hands when they attempted to begin an attack upon hearing faint cries from the women. "It is better our women be soiled than dead," he said. "What shall we do, White Mouse?"

"The rest is up to you, my friend," White Mouse said. "I only brought you here."

The attack was as artless and as old as the plains. The warriors killed the sentries with silent ferocity as soon as it was dark, then crept into the camp and over a dozen of the strangers lay dead before an outcry was raised. The others were herded into a group around the rebuilt central fire, stripped of their clothing, tied to the ground with rawhide fixed to stakes, and burned. The camp was methodically looted, the valuable copper and brass cooking pots stowed in the wagons for the return to the mesa, the firearms thrown into the river on orders of the Warrior-Chief, everything burnable added to the fire. When they left, before daylight, the only remaining trace of the strangers' camp was the smouldering corpses, which would be picked clean and the bones scattered within another day.

⎯⎯⎯⎯⎯▷ ◁⎯⎯⎯⎯⎯

After the ceremonial rites for the dead, there was an impromptu three-day celebration on the mesa when the tribe was again united. At its height, the tribal chief called for quiet and announced that he was relinquishing his position as chief in shame, believing he was responsible for leading the men away while the strangers took their women. An admission of disgrace was a solemn and sobering thing; the people waited to hear what the chief would say next. "Leadership belongs with those who will lead wisely and well. I ask you to name White Mouse as chief and spiritual leader in my stead."

And so matters rested for a day, giving the people opportunity to mull over this development, and to give the elders time to prepare their inquisition for White Mouse, asking him in public assembly why he thought he could lead the people, and how he planned to accomplish it. The spontaneity was gone from the celebration the following night and the people gathered in the ceremonial place were serious and concerned. The chief again made his formal renunciation and stepped to join the crowd, symbolizing that he would forever be but one of them.

White Mouse moved as if to prevent the chief from going, then faced his people. "I cannot question the actions of the man who has had the loyalty of his people for so long. I can only say I find no fault in my heart toward a man who was betrayed by strangers who came to him posing as friends." The crowd nodded and murmured, several of them passing choice bits of food to the self-deposed chief.

"Although I am now a man in my body," White Mouse went on, "I do not feel I have either the instinct or industry to lead you as your chief." There were a few dissenting shouts. Most, however, waited. "There is one among us who is admired and respected by all, a man who has already proven himself to be a leader. With all the respect my youth can offer, I suggest you name the Warrior-Chief as leader of this tribe from this time forward." After but a brief moment of silence, this speech was greeted with applause and the Warrior-Chief was pushed forward. The elders, now relieved of their private misgivings about White Mouse's youth, seconded the suggestion by installing the Warrior-Chief without the traditional inquisition.

⎯⎯⎯⎯⎯▷ ◁⎯⎯⎯⎯⎯

Several months later the chief visited White Mouse in his new house, grumbling as he squeezed his bulk past the offset wall by the door. "I will regret having this place built for you if I am trapped in here," he said.

"You will notice my entrance-way keeps the snow from my bed," White Mouse said. He indicated the fireplace in the corner. "Warm yourself."

"What instrument of the underworld is this?" the chief said, stooping to examine the warm glowing fire built into an oven-like opening protruding from a corner of the single room.

"It is an idea I took from the minds of the strangers while we were burning them." He sighed. "But I cannot persuade the others to do likewise, nor can I get the women to use the metal pots for cooking."

"Ah, White Mouse, you cannot alter the habits of the ages in a single lifetime. We have the good life now and we older ones can see no reason to change it."

White Mouse moved to squat beside the chief at the fire. "Then why do you send the young boys to me for spiritual instruction?"

"That is in retaliation for your having me named tribal chief. Besides, the Great One could never penetrate this thick skull of mine. My place is to lead the hunts in summer and break heads when the idle winter brings boredom and quarrels." The chief gazed long into the fire. "I hear strange reports of your teachings."

"If you disapprove, why did you wait so long to come to me?"

"Have I said a word about disapproving? Perhaps I, myself, am not really too old to learn new things if it will better the lot of our people."

Taking a stick, White Mouse dipped two steaming strips of meat from the pot by the fire and stretched them on a clean board to cool before offering them to the chief. "I do not think of myself as a teacher," he said slowly. "I only try to lead the boys to see that which I can see."

"But you are a prophet gifted by the Great One," the chief said. "How can you transfer this gift to lesser minds?"

White Mouse had pondered through many silent nights on the nature of his gift. One did not question the reasons why the gift had been bestowed; it was simply there and must be used as the Great One lighted the path. But he sometimes ground his teeth in frustration as he almost remembered another life where he had been more adequately trained in the use of the gift. For the span of a breath he would feel himself in a strange, flowing garment and in that instant the air in his lungs would be icy, colder even than the brittle winters of his home mountains. As suddenly as it appeared, the vision was gone and he would rub his hand over his head in exasperation, sometimes wondering at his mild surprise at finding thick hair instead of a shaven pate.

"By using the tools at hand," he finally said in answer to the chief's question. "For example, you will lead us to the fields when we plant our grain to invoke the spirits to bring us tall grain and to keep the river running full and bountiful during the hot season. Do you know why you do this?"

"Why. . . it is part of our ritual. I would not think of offending the spirits of the fields and water."

"But do you secretly believe our harvest would be just as plentiful without this ritual?" White Mouse persisted.

"I cannot tell you because I do not know."

"Well, I can tell you it would not be plentiful. It is therefore my duty to lead the people to see and know these spirits. . . to love them even as we love each other as brothers."

"Have you seen these spirits, White Mouse?"

"Yes."

The chief lowered his voice. "Have you seen the Great One himself?"

White Mouse took a deep breath and smiled. "I see the Great One every day. I see him in you because you have life. I see him in the birds above us and in the grains that grow to feed us. I know he lives because I live."

The chief took a strip of meat in his fingers and ate it slowly. "This shows you I am willing to learn," he said. "I am eating your meat which was cooked in water. The taste would be better without the salt." He licked his fingers. "But I cannot understand this business of the Great One existing as the spirit of all life. It makes no sense. I had best return to settling squabbles between women who quarrel over the ownership of dogs."

"Come with me to the mountains when the snow is gone," White Mouse said. "Perhaps there the Great One will reveal himself to you more clearly."

"Ha!" the chief said. "You are no better than the women who gather atop the highest house to chant for the dead, believing that by being higher they are nearer to the Great One."

White Mouse laughed and began to eat his own strip of meat. "One very practical reason for going to the mountains is to escape the chatter of women. . . and old men whose feet are mired in buffalo dung."

The Chief stood, "Very well, I will go to your precious mountains with you but I warn you, I will believe only what I see." He paused in the doorway. "Buffalo dung, indeed!"

White Mouse was still chuckling when Wild Witch came in, her movements so fluid and effortless he was hardly aware of her until she squatted beside him. "You were long," he said. "Was it difficult?"

She snorted. "The mother was difficult. She threshed around so much the baby came late and was not breathing."

"It was dead?" He reached for her, knowing the private torments she suffered when delivering a dead baby.

She pulled away from him, laughing. "Oh, the baby is fine now. I breathed my own life into it."

He smiled. "The last time you did that, they named the baby for you."

"They did this time, too. Which is just as well, since you don't seem to have much success in making me babies of my own." She took a vessel and left the house to bring water from the roof. He heard her as she climbed the ladder and then the faint thumping as she removed the covering from the reservoir he had built around the chimney to keep the water and snow melted in winter.

He watched her as she stripped her clothing off and began to bathe, the sight of her warming him with pleasure as it always did. "Do the women still believe you to be possessed of evil because you bathe in the cold season?"

She shrugged. "They don't speak to me of it. They know now I will not deliver the babies or treat the sick until I wash them." She gave him an impish grin. "I tell them the word to wash comes directly from the Great One through you. They don't really believe me but they'd rather undergo a bath than take the chance that I might be telling the truth."

"You are shameless," he said. "I will beat you when the weather is more suitable. In the meantime, bring your clean body to me and I will try again to make you a baby."

<hr>

The years assembled and Wild Witch brought her own babies into the world. She trained them in work and responsibility and sent the males early with the other boys to go with White Mouse to absorb the wisdom of the fields, the waters and the high places. Prompted by a voice which told her it was now time, she went with White Mouse to the high places and fasted with only water and berries of the wild rose for the full passage of a moon and returned with the knowledge of healing which she laid on the sick with her hands.

As time passed, the Wild Witch's fame spread through the knowledge/awareness known to all open to the universal embrace of the Great One. Few persons questioned this; it came as naturally as breathing. Those who nurtured doubt and suspicion left their clans and tribes and spent their lives in lonely, wandering privation.

Winter was ending when hunters who had wintered in the warmer southern deserts met three young runners who were too ill to run further. They had come from the place where the seas from the east and seas from the west sought to meet and mate, separated by a narrow steaminess of jungle less than a half moon's walk from sea to sea.

The runners were the strongest of a dozen who had begun the journey to the biting northern cold to seek out the Healing Woman. They left a great nation whose numbers were dying so swiftly their bodies could no longer be buried or even burned. The twelve were whole of body when their journey began but the sickness came with them as a cloud. As they dropped and could go no further they drew themselves apart and sought to conceal the suppurating sores that marred their bodies overnight. With sadness but understanding more fully the urgency of their trek, their companions left them to die alone and continued northward, foraging only enough to hold their strength, stopping only when exhaustion dropped them. They would awaken and continue, occasionally pausing to hear the death song of a comrade whose temporal life span was now ending.

When they found them, the mesa hunters with their horses quickly brought the survivors to the foot of the mesa and echoed the urgency of their need to the Wild Witch above. She hurried down, camped them all near the river and let none approach while she worked unceasing days and nights to suppress the dreaded contagion brought to the southern people by another expedition of strangers from beyond the seas. The Wild Witch's eyes grew dark, remembering the death the same strangers had visited upon her own people. The world was larger than she had thought, and it was changing.

The three strangers died in a few days while the hunters gagged on the bitter remedies the Wild One forced on them, swearing darkly but privately and among themselves because they were being kept from their women and the festivities they anticipated after months of absence. But the disease did not touch them.

Knowing she was not infected, she returned to the mesa and told White Mouse, "I must go." White Mouse held her, even as he knew they were already separated as she swiftly and methodically inventoried her vast knowledge of healing. Over her head, he signaled to their oldest son who left and returned in minutes with the chief.

The chief squatted for an hour at the fire, sorting and organizing the fragments of conversation the Wild One hurled at them in her haste to be gone. She stripped and ritually bathed herself, totally unself-conscious of her body, reciting aloud what was to be done. Her mate, her chief and her children remained silent and motionless. Knowing she would only be out in the cold a few days as they moved southward, she packed efficiently and lightly, knowing she would find the healing offerings of the Earth Mother enroute. She stood and smiled radiantly at those she loved most. "I will go now". To the chief, "I need three horses."

"We will leave at first light," the chief said.

"I will leave now," she said, black fire in her eyes.

"You are letting your heart speak. You must contain the spirit before we depart." The chief looked full at her, his expression unchanging. "We will leave at first light."

She scathed the chief with another look which caused even White Mouse to avert his eyes. Then she sank to her knees, the fire in her eyes receding but strong enough to hold the others in stillness. "Tell me," she said.

"I know of this land," the chief said. "It will be hard, but with me you will reach it in less than a moon. It would take far longer if you took only those you are teaching to be carriers of the Light. Rest this night, seek and build more firmly the totems of your spirit-mind. Meet me at the foot of the mesa at first light." Without seeming to hurry, he was gone.

Not commenting, the chief allowed his little expedition of twenty strong men and extra horses to be led for two days almost non-stop by the Healing Witch. The chief knew that most of the younger tribal members spoke of her in these terms even though, linguistically, it smacked of sacrilege and was only voiced in whispers. "Witch" and "Wild Witch" came easily to most because her bubbling energy always overflowed and the mischief never left her eyes during the century that life pulsed in her body. But the term "Witch Healer" was sanctified in varying degrees by all and used in hesitant jest by the young with the vague naughtiness of adolescents testing the equivalent of their first swear words in a language as then uncluttered with profanity.

The chief acceded to the initial urgency for different reasons. He knew their greater physical strength must be utilized in getting his party southward through the still frigid highlands quickly, unencumbered by women and hunters' tepees dragged on triangular wooden devices behind the horses. The chief also knew that other tribes who survived the cold by pillaging others would be in the lands they were to cross. By staying in motion the chief hoped his small group would discourage the little scouting parties of marauding tribes he occasionally glimpsed in the distance. A compact party obviously traveling in a purposeful way would hopefully not be worth raiding. Settling his weariness into his rump astride his horse, the chief chuckled deep in his belly. He would never understand how White Mouse had communicated this information to him about the risks they would face in the few moments it took him to counter the Wild Witch's demands the night before they left. He wouldn't ask White Mouse. He had done this before and gotten the smiling answer that if he already knew the answer, what difference did the 'how' make.

On the third day the Wild Witch's horse refused to let her mount and the escort had angrily camped half a mile away to build fires, rest and roast a doe they had surprised and killed in the early morning. Warming her softened leather garments over the fire so they would better absorb the unguents she'd brought to repel the increasing vermin found in the warmer climates, she flipped a skirt at the chief's face. "Do you want me to admit now that my knowledge and power are inadequate for this? Is this why you insisted on coming with me?" The chief remained silent as she tried to warm herself by wrapping up in a stiff buffalo-hide sleeping robe. She gave her body up to physical weariness and slept with her head resting on her knees.

When they reached the afflicted land, not even the Wild Witch was prepared for the misery which awaited them. The nation had divided itself into two camps, the sick and the not-sick. The sick were driven out into the jungles and during the half year the sickness had raged, the sick had built their own survival community. Opening her mind to guidance, the Wild Witch found many in the outcast villages who had recovered from the illness but were not permitted to return to their homes scarred and weakened.

Acting swiftly and without stopping to reason, she asked the chief to withdraw blood from the palms and wrists of those who were healed, using as her reason the universally understood blood-bonding of tribes. Congealing the blood into a sticky mass under the humid tropical sun, she took it to the still healthy but panicky city. She appropriated the sunniest, most spacious walled enclosure normally used for religious ceremonies and ordered the newly-sick to be brought to her.

Chanting softly, she applied the blood of the healed ones, now made into an ointment with clay and oil, to the new sores on healthy bodies. Many of her patients sickened and died, their final agonies relieved by teas she brewed from dark green leaves, bright flowers after they shed their petals and the knobby heart of a stubby cactus she found in abundance. Others became well, and then more.

The way was hard and she had little time for patience or tenderness. Those who had prayed for her coming now ran away to make the sign to protect them from the evil eye when they met her. She paid no attention but continued with her work, recruiting those now healed (the "scarred ones") to help her. Seeing that it made her work easier, she let the word spread that the healed ones were now somehow touched with her supernatural powers when the disease ceased to spread after another half a year and the surviving outcasts were cautiously allowed to return home.

To give impetus to the frightened natives, the chief marched his troops into a massive night-long fire dance. The non-sick came when they were assured they would be separated from the sick by an intense fire of hardwood logs. The chief's men, many sullen and with dried blood still forming scabs from hard-handed blows to the head and shoulders which the chief assured them was the gentlest persuasion he would use, stepped resolutely into the fire circle to meet with equal numbers of the sick-who-had-become-well. The Wild Witch passed between them, slashing each palm lightly with an obsidian blade and urging each individual to join his blood with the other. None of the mesa people sickened.

Through meditation and a brief fast, the Wild Witch perceived that the entire populace would have to be innoculated. Dismayed by the enormity of this task, she climbed the huge, squat pyramid in the city's center with the chief and asked his help. She chose the pyramid as the one place where she could find privacy. She saw it was a holy place because it was deserted. Using universal signs and her growing vocabulary of the new language, she learned the pyramid could only be scaled when led by a high priest on special days. The priests had all died during the great sickness so she never learned its significance but was gratified that her healing powers had granted her a deification of some sort so the people made no objection when she climbed the pyramid every few days to meditate and, most importantly, to rest.

"Why don't you call the White Mouse with your mind?" the chief said, stalling for time as he studied the geometric precision of the city below them. Wide avenues with great trees in their centers radiated from the pyramid's base and seemed to blend into the green haze of the jungle in the near distance.

He knew sadness as he realized the architects of this great city were long dead and their memories were being eroded as surely as the summer rains forced more tough roots under the already lumpy pavements.

"Isn't it enough that you left White Mouse with our own people to rule?" she said, letting the conversation develop on a relaxing tone. "They still become more obedient children before your brute force than they do at his gentle wisdom."

The chief pondered, his mind expanding with amused love as his memory filed favorite episodes into categories. "Did the Mouse tell you he once threw me three times over-the-head when we were angry at ourselves for finding no new game to kill?"

She laughed and it was a good feeling after the months of tension. "You know the White Mouse tells me nothing of his own life. Although we are one, we must tread separate paths."

"It is enough to know I am of the family," the chief said. They sat and watched the brief blaze of sunset and shared the wonder of the tropical darkness which came with the suddenness of a woman throwing a blanket over the lamp to quiet restless children. "But you know the answer," he said, scraping flint to iron to create a smudge fire to keep away mosquitos that thickened near them.

"But you are the chief," she said, teasing.

"I am also an honorary high priest because you dragged me up to this place." He sighed. "They will only listen to me because I am a man, even though they know the wisdom comes from you."

She turned sorrowing eyes to the north. "Our own people need us and we must return soon after the rains have stopped here. All healing blood must be mixed before we go."

The chief sat silent for an hour, studying the glittering sky. He groaned under his breath, knowing he must make a long speech. He waved an arm in a useless gesture and began. "In less time than the span of my fingers the moon you cannot now see will thin himself, disappear and return facing the other sky. All people seem to know the change means new life. We plant our seeds in the ground and the bellies of women at this time for a more bountiful harvest. I will take the new authority you have given me and proclaim a festival where all beings must blend their blood one with another." He got heavily to his feet, a giant and powerful yet troubled man. "You will tell me what to do when the time is right." It was a question.

She smiled up at him. "The time will be in five days, very early in the day, when the young moon rises to face the sun before he appears. Be ready and I will be ready."

Interrupted only by the crying of sleepy children, the blending of blood ceremony was orchestrated by the Wild Witch with a smoothness the chief quickly recognized she had been rehearsing in the form of games for weeks beforehand. Unwillingly but with the sober counseling of the chief, she appointed a new government so she and the chief could return to their home with their entourage before a new winter made the journey impossible.

To save face the chief raged at the third of his men who insisted on remaining in the land of steamy sunshine to enjoy the more relaxed mating practices of the southern people. He loved his young men and envied them in a remote way but sternly took their horses from them. The chief left an aging stallion in exchange for a nearly grown pair of black skinned slaves whose color and docile temperament caught his fancy. At Wild Witch's suggestion, he also left a young brood mare so the pyramid people, as they now called them, could try to form their own herd. Happily, the chief never learned his precious horses were slaughtered and eaten before the next moon transited the heavens.

Back at the mesas, the adolescent black couple relished the hot, dry summer but were useless objects of abject discomfort during the time of the winds and snow. The blacks went through another summer cheerfully enough but none of the mesa people were surprised when the blacks trotted proudly off to the south and west on their dearly earned ponies when the first hard chill hardened the ground underfoot, signaling the onset of another high country winter.

True to his word, the chief went with White Mouse and his boys to the mountains. If he experienced revelation or ecstasy he revealed it to no man but nevertheless continued the annual pilgrimage until age bent and twisted his legs to where he could not scale the heights. No proclamation was ever made, but in the solemn sittings of the council, White Mouse always sat silently by his chief's side. Following one such meeting which had lasted a day and a night and well into the next day, the chief sent for Wild Witch to lay her hands on his body to ease the pain which sought to consume him. Waiting in exhaustion, the chief talked. "I will not go to the heights with you this year, White Mouse. Nor will I go again. This body is nearing its finish."

"My young ones will carry you," White Mouse said.

"It is not seemly for a chief to be carried. Nor is it seemly for a man to remain chief when he is lame and old and infirm." The chief tried to straighten his legs and groaned. "You have ruled with me for many years. Will you now have me carried once more to the high places and left. . . and then rule for me?"

"Our village is becoming a city," White Mouse said. "There are nearly two thousand of us, according to the spring counting. I am a man of spirit, not of human judgment. I would suggest taking your oldest son and my oldest son for a fast period and then present them to the elders for the inquisition at the time of the harvest dance."

"Ah, White Mouse, they have neither my experience nor your wisdom," the chief said.

"They have patience and intelligence," White Mouse said. "Your son is forty, mine is thirty. They have taken part in our rituals since their initiations. If we have not guided them well by this time we have failed. You say you are old, and I agree, but remember that I have also lived more than half a hundred years and will not have that many more to look forward to."

"True, true," the chief said. "Where is that wretched woman of yours! I am in pain and need her."

White Mouse laughed at him. "You are reverting to your younger days, old friend. Compare your suffering now to that you endured on your first trip with me to the high places."

The chief lay back and remembered. Asking no deference to his age or position, he had trotted with the boys up and down the mesa, bringing water. This was to teach that the first duty of man was to serve his fellow man, and to serve with the most life-giving commodity at hand. . . water. Then they bathed in the river and rested in the sweet grass, inhaling the fragrance and taking new life from the earth, mother of all. In the hour before sunset they toured the village, marking their footprints in the dust, touching the stones of the houses man had made, gazing deeply into the faces of parents and friends, noting and memorizing the burial places of ancestors, taking final stock of man and his works.

At sundown White Mouse began the march to the precipice which, he knew, would be lighted when the full moon moved past the spire called the Spider Woman. He had taught them to breathe on earlier marches so the all-night climb was more therapeutic than an ordeal. White Mouse discouraged conversation during the climb. The more thoughtful of the group gave this religious significance. After a few hours of exertion, most recognized the practicality of rhythmic breathing, which would be interrupted by talk.

In the false dawn when the moon had completed its arc and the promise of the sun threw a silver-black reflection on the sky, White Mouse halted his young men on a scrubby area and let them rest.

Many slept, hunched against each other for warmth. They became restless as daylight began, those who had not brought water nagging others who had thought to bring skins of water slung over their shoulders. They quieted and the chief made his way to where White Mouse sat on a boulder shadowed by the Spider Woman and overlooking the route they had taken and the mesa and village below. "What did you do?" White Mouse said. "Beat them unconscious?"

"No," the chief said. "I told them you were communing with the Great One. What are you doing, by the way?"

White Mouse massaged the calves of his legs. "To tell the truth, I'm trying to figure out what to do next."

"I thought you were supposed to be inspired and uplifted when we got here."

"I am," White Mouse said. "I just don't know how to communicate it. Don't you feel something, just being here?"

"I feel tired," the chief said. "And my feet hurt."

They sat, not speaking, until the sun reached the mountain. White Mouse stood and the chief stood with him. "Give the call," White Mouse said.

The chief filled his lungs with the thin air and began the chant, older than memory, to invoke the favor of the Great One and bring all souls into peaceful harmony. His voice, pitched high, rose and fell and the boys stirred and walked toward them. At the appropriate time they joined the prayer and then were quiet.

White Mouse stood and waited, a slight smile on his face as he felt the invisible forces of the eons begin to pour into his body. He spread his arms, his hands extended to the boys. Some stepped back, then the group surged together, touching each other. When White Mouse spoke his voice took on a resonance the others had not heard. "My brothers, we are not here to view the new and the miraculous. We are here to open our eyes to the spirit in which we all live. I have shown you the water, of which the mother earth herself must drink to live. I have shown you the grain and the foods of the earth with which we make our bread. I have taught you to love the animals which we must kill so that we, the stronger, may survive. I have shown you that man must build; I have shown you the burial grounds to illustrate to you that the body must always die. I bring you here to show you the futility of man aspiring to immortality through his own works. Look down. See the way you have traveled during the night. See the village where you have spent your lives."

Crowding each other, the group moved to look down. "Now look up," White Mouse commanded. "Is there a limit to what you can see? Looking down, you are limited. You see in the breadth of a finger what we have built in a thousand years. You see in the mountains what the wind and waters have built in a million years. But you are looking up now and you see no end. So it is with the spirit. You will not end. You will grow, and as you grow, the spirit will grow." White Mouse moved to recall attention to himself. "We will stay here this day. Those of you who have brought food, do not eat it. Those who have brought water, share it, but sparingly. We will not sleep this night, but watch the stars as they pass above us. At the next sunrise, we will descend, and we will descend as men."

White Mouse walked among them during the night. Those who slept he roused and sent alone down the mountain. For those who ate, he made them inhale the smoke of burning feathers and they vomited. Those who returned down the mountains during the third day chanted with fervor, for one of their comrades who had been sent from the group for sleeping had fallen and died while descending the mountain.

⎯⎯⎯⎯⎯◄►⎯⎯⎯⎯⎯

The Wild Witch returned and rubbed the old chief's legs with an oil boiled from a plant she had found in the lowlands by the river. "Our chief wants to be taken to the wild lands to die," White Mouse said. "The way is long. Can you prepare his legs for such a journey?"

"Nonsense," Wild Witch said. "His legs will not carry him and he is too heavy to be dragged. We will take him to his own house and I will prepare the potion."

The old chief heaved himself to his knees. "You only give the potion to those of sick minds who might poison the others," he shouted. "I will go in my own way and in my own time."

"Then why must we shout at each other?" Wild Witch said, wrapping oil-saturated cloths around the old man's legs. "An old man with this much evil in him will probably live for another century."

His pain eased, the old chief sent Wild Witch to bring his sons to carry him to his house. "You know the times and circumstances," he said. "Have I reached the end of this life?"

"You have been to the mountain with me for thirty years," White Mouse said. "Have you learned nothing?"

The old chief stared at White Mouse with his still-clear black eyes and scratched his chest with dry, raspy fingers. "How does one learn what one already knows? The mountain gave me life. Now I can no longer go to the mountain so I do not desire more life." He grinned at his friend, in perfect understanding. "We will call the council and have a dance with the next full moon and name our sons as leaders of our people."

The old chief died in the season of the sowing of the grain. He passed surrounded by the warriors he had trained, hearing the cadenced thrumming of the drums and the muted wailing of the women in the background. White Mouse stayed with him until the end, and accompanied the chief's etheric essence to the transitional phase to make the introductions before returning to the tribe to lead them in a funeral ceremonial memorable enough to take its place as legend through the following generation.

In accordance with his request and in deference to the honor due him for his many years of leadership, the chief's body was carried to the wilderness to be returned to the elements. The final leg of the journey was made by the sons of the chief and White Mouse, bearing the chief's body another full day into the tortured wasteland. The young men returned smiling and suffused with an almost tangible aura of peace. They were regarded with awe by the others because they alone had participated in a ceremony so sacred it might never be known in a lifetime.

⸺ ⊃ ⊂ ⸺

White Mouse lived far longer than he had anticipated. Through the years, he paused to contemplate his death and to prepare his spiritual self for a suitable transition. Tribal quarrels, crop failures and sweeping epidemics of sickness filled his life and that of his Wild Witch so he grumblingly postponed his own end until this or that problem of his people could be resolved. He traveled far with the Wild Witch, opening his body in ways he did not attempt to understand to the forces which his woman took from him to heal and bring comfort to those who needed them. Others of his kind from lands to the south where the snows never came made their pilgrimages and brought to his people the wonderful mathematical calendar which measured the passage of the sun, stars and moon to form time into years. Comprehending this device with grudging admiration, White Mouse reckoned his years as approaching a hundred so he relinquished the spirit within him to leave a now aching and creaking body.

Full summer had baked the earth to stone when White Mouse grumpily refused the breakfast Wild Witch had prepared him. He sat on the ground with his back against his house for an hour, then re-entered the house. "Ah, Ancient Woman, even the sun can no longer warm these old bones." She did not speak but watched with alert eyes as he settled himself onto his pallet again. "I think at the end of three days I will depart this hulk for the better place we know so well."

She moved to him and put her hands on him. He chuckled, a raspy, papery sound. "No, I have no pain, nor will there be any. The temptation is strong to leave within the hour but I cannot deny those we love the luxury of their mourning. It is good I have become so deaf I will not have to undergo the wailings of the women. Let us rest together till sundown and then you will call our sons and the elders." She nodded and lay beside him. Words between them had been unnecessary for many years and since his deafness she seldom bothered to speak to him, letting him talk as he would, knowing that the saying of words still brought him pleasure.

The mourning began that evening, ritualistically yet with an intensity remembered by none then living. Men left the groups of chanters singly and wept alone, or came to stare long at White Mouse's house, as if by force of their love to make him young and virile again. Either through a mistake in his calculations or utter weariness, shortly after sundown of the second day, White Mouse closed his eyes and stopped breathing.

The Healers, all taught their arts by Wild Witch, deferred to her and drew back as she called his name loudly in one ear and then the other, a suspicion of a smile forming new patterns in the thousand wrinkles of her face as she thought of his years-long deafness. She rose and faced the crowded room. "He is indeed dead!" she said. "We will leave him alone this night so the Great One may come for his spirit in the privacy and dignity he has earned."

It was late before the village slept, exhausted by telling and re-telling the wonders of White Mouse, who had lived to become a legend in his own lifetime. Sensing that which he could not hear, White Mouse opened his eyes and forced enough air into his lungs to lend a ponderous pulse to his almost dormant heart. Slowly, slowly, he arose and walked outside. He stood for many minutes, gazing serenely at the blaze of stars in the moonless sky. He lay on his back and, still watching the stars, listened with deep contentment as his heart again slowed and finally stopped. It was there his people found him in the morning, and the story was repeated countless thousands of times about the Great White Mouse, so beloved by the Great One himself that the Great One had moved the body to the solitary splendor of the desert night to take its soul.

The discussion of White Mouse's final resting place had begun during the final hours of his life and when his stiffened body was found outside the words came to all lips, "The High Place!" Every male volunteered. A dozen of the strongest and most daring were chosen. The body of White Mouse was reverently wrapped and tied securely to a litter which was hauled by incredible effort to the uppermost reaches of the needle of stone called the Spider Woman and there left to the elements from which he had gained and taught such strength.

The following day a hundred-year-old woman walked slowly but with purpose through the village, nodding and speaking pleasantly to all whom she met. The word went before her, carried by scurrying children. "The Wild Witch is going out," the old ones said. "The Ancient Woman is going," said the younger. As she left the village to begin the descent from the mesa, a few women ran timidly into the road to touch her, others lifted their children to see her.

Many eyes watched throughout the day as Wild Witch trudged into the shimmering distance and into the mountains from which they knew she would not return. And a silence which covers a grief and loss too profound for expression settled on the village.

There were tears in our eyes as we re-lived the final days of White Mouse and his Wild Witch. A deep sense of gratitude approaching reverence filled us to be shown anew lives of usefulness and service, lives during which our spirits expanded and grew, advancing another step in the inexorable progression toward a fuller unity with the Infinite.

Keetoowah just chuckled, lit another Kool and coughed. "You kids really had a time for yourselves," he said. We grinned at each other and I barely restrained myself from saying, "How, Chief", and extending my right palm to his, not touching, but only to ensure our vibrations were in harmony.

I looked affectionately at the big Indian sitting cross-legged on a huge pillow on our living room floor. Enjoying a leisurely visit, it was easy to focus my consciousness on another time and see my friend Keetoowah as the iron-muscled Warrior Chief who had become the mesa people's most potent tribal chief in generations. He was even bigger then, towering over six feet of sinewy toughness which enabled him to scramble up the mountain as agilely as many of the teen-aged boys we led until he must have been well into his eighties. Age wasn't measured in years then but we both have a strong feeling that Keetoowah lived about a hundred and ten years. This was not unusual because the old were revered and protected.

The wisest men became tribal elders but any old man could be assured a respectful audience even if his stories were repeated a hundred times. Old women, with a sort of grim glee, were often tyrants to the younger wives and maids.

Another fragment triggered a memory and he eyed us with baleful contemplation. "Yeah, I also remember you guys and your eagle-watching. You couldn't have been over eleven or twelve. I yelled my guts out at you to get down off that cliff and get back to work in the fields."

I remembered, too, and had a momentary guilt pang as I recalled our taunting him to come up and get us. He still reads me as easily as a newspaper, and he grinned a little. He had been more fearful we'd fall than he was outraged. Closing my eyes to see again the almost sheer 100-meter cliff we were on, I felt a remnant of a quiver in my own middle-aged bones.

At the outset we were awed by the task we had undertaken, to live again entire lifetimes. The saga of White Mouse required only a few days to write. The Poet selected periods in our lives which would invoke key memories and dictated a few pages of notes. The expanding of these notes took longer because with each phase a vibrant set of recollections was set into being and I could 'see' myself as White Mouse as clearly as I remember scenes from my own childhood. . . or even ten years ago. The real chore came in searching out the WHY of past lifetimes, the reasons which compelled us to return again and again to this earthly plane although we knew that lives of far greater beauty and serenity were available to us in other areas of existence.

The specific WHY of our many earth experiences is not now available to anyone, even to us in our present awareness. We can only surmise that it is encompassed in the person of a more developed entity, of which our current earthly life is but a fragment. Therefore, we must take the lifetime as we recalled it and work backward in an effort to discern a pattern which may appear in several lifetimes and, most important, can be tied to the present one. One could say the method is one of working from effect to cause.

We have a particular warmth toward the lives of White Mouse and Wild Witch because even as children they were open to and aware of a higher spirituality. Since we believe reincarnation is an elective process, it follows that these lives were planned with great care so that when they came into being on earth they would be in the best position to get together. This makes a very practical sort of sense. That race of people loosely grouped into the term 'Indian' are more intimately attuned to the combined forces of the spirit than the white man.

Pursuing logical conjecture, the mated souls concluded the probabilities were good that they would accomplish their mission by appearing at the same time in an isolated Indian village. They knew in advance they would in all likelihood not have recall of other lifetimes to guide them; as indeed they did not, except for White Mouse's occasional flashes of another life perhaps spent in Tibet, and which will be related later, although I have no way of knowing if White Mouse shared the memory of the same lifetime I do. They also knew before birth the chances of failure. They could have absorbed some genetic trait which, in the invariable exercise of free will, might have led them away from each other. Alone, either could have accomplished much but together, they changed the face of their little world to where a sometimes-recalled legend of the "beautiful ones" still lives.

As a matter of incidental interest, five years after completing the original manuscript, our oldest daughter sent us a copy of an article she had found in an obscure academic publication. The article recounted a legend told by today's descendants of the "Mesa people". This folk tale details the life of a venerated tribal patriarch known as White Mouse.

We have not been able to return in conscious memory to the periods between lifetimes. This information is within our subjective consciousness and I have tapped it occasionally under the hands of highly qualified hypnotists and once, foolishly, through an inexpert experiment with self hypnosis which almost ended in disaster. As stated earlier, Carol is not now amenable to hypnosis, and no qualified practitioner was available to me during this writing. So we do not know if White Mouse and Wild Witch did accomplish what they planned prior to that lifetime. We can see the obvious, however, that the two lives united as a single loving unit succeeded in giving far in excess of what they took. And with this we are content.

III

The satisfaction of viewing a lifetime well spent is great but brings bemused speculation. . . if it was all that great, why have we returned to earth several times since then? The lives of White Mouse and Wild Witch were good, but they represented only one successful step forward. Success is a heady thing, it encourages one to emulate and repeat it. Our next opportunity to share a lifetime prior to the present one occurred less than a hundred years ago. We had been together as father and daughter in the late 18th-century Paris, I, an apparently conservative university professor, had felt compelled to place my strong-willed daughter (Carol) in a covent at an early age. We had other lives in the interim but they were so widely divergent from each other that it seems we had not tried to be together.

About 1875 an only son was born to a wealthy coal mine owner in Wales. The plentitude of money coupled with the father's almost paranoic ambition for his son pushed the son far beyond his native abilities. He was privately and intensively tutored until of an age where he was entered in university for formal medical training. Upon receiving his medical degree he was enabled, by virtue of his father's wealth, to spend several years with various famous doctors on the Continent. This experience polished him and gave him an easy facility with languages but left him woefully lacking in the dedicated Hippocratic concept of the practice of medicine.

When he was 30, the young doctor's father purchased for him a fashionable, outrageously expensive practice in London. It was the father's fondest hope that, with such a start, the son would eventually be recognized and knighted by the court. This did not happen but the doctor's position was such that, when he volunteered his services at the outbreak of World War I he was appointed a Colonel in the Medical Services and at the time of his death in 1917 was a Brigadier.

Although the doctor had an exaggerated opinion of himself, he was astute enough to recognize that he needed competent assistants. He chose as his office nurse a woman near his own age who had been raised and trained by the truly great English physician whose practice he had bought.

His nurse was the most valuable addition the doctor was to make to his staff. She was an intimate of many noble households in a professional capacity, was highly respected and knew a great deal more about medicine than her employer.

It was the nurse who descreetly suggested second opinions on difficult cases, who manipulated the actual work of more able men to where her doctor gained the ultimate acclaim. She always knew he was a fraud but when, after five years of employment, he asked her to marry him, she did. She was probably never easy within herself as merely the wife of a noted doctor for, when he entered the military in 1915 she returned to her nursing and maintained his offices with a staff of young, seriously dedicated physicians.

Ironically, the doctor's only act of real significance was his own death, by suicide in 1917. In a mission more notable for stupidity than bravery, he had himself put ashore with five commandos in northern Germany with some vague notion of effecting the release of a group of high-ranking Allied officers being held in secure and comfortable imprisonment in Hamburg. He had relied on his not quite adequate knowledge of the German language plus his familiarity with the territory to carry it off and had used his rank to get the fiasco underway without the knowledge of his superiors. They were captured almost immediately, barely having time to shed their outer clothing to reveal their uniforms underneath so they would not be shot forthwith as spies.

Unfortunately, the doctor's rank of Brigadier had given him privy to a great deal more secret military information than he had any business knowing. The Germans were delighted with the capture of a general officer and made no secret to the doctor that they planned a most intensive interrogation. It is doubtful that they would have employed physical torture but the intimation of it was enough to unman the doctor, force him to take perhaps his first honest inventory of himself and then to sever his femoral artery and quietly bleed to death. It would have taken little persuasion for him to reveal everything he knew.

It is not known if the doctor's wife learned of his death. She died of influenza within a short time of his passing.

A reconstruction of these lives shows a familiar pattern of planning. In spirit, I would have been aware of the Welshman's single-minded desire to sire a son who would become a doctor. By the same token, Carol could have placed herself in the world in a position where the probabilities were high that she would become a professional nurse. It would be a compatible occupation for her, one which she had already experienced any number of times in prior lifetimes.

To be sure, this is guesswork and doesn't have many elements of credibility. If we could sift the details I'm sure that that particular meeting and mating was accomplished under more precise and exacting circumstances.

Quite possibly we met in other realms of consciousness and applied some kind of psychic leverage to promising situations. I do know we have been guided and led during our lives, many times. However it came about, we met and mated. . .but failed.

WHY? In a classic example of the exercise of free will, the doctor assumed a position he had neither earned nor merited, simply because it was easy and pleasant. He contributed nothing, so nothing accrued to him. The nurse made a much more promising beginning but again, the ease of wealth and position was too much to resist after a life until now filled with hard, albeit rewarding, work.

It would be easy to condemn the officiously incompetent doctor to oblivion and say good riddance. But that doctor not only was but is me. The memory still lives of the stomach-tightening uncertainty of the doctor as he frowned at the charts on his desk, totally unable to make a diagnosis. I can feel the familiar clammy sweats as he searched for something to say to a condescending, aristocratic patient. These are uneasy recollections because that most recent past lifetime is in so many ways superimposed on my current life. They have also been a tremendous help. I am still plagued by indecisiveness but being able to predict my probable behavior under conditions of stress has given me strength and greater assurance.

Keetoowah and I try to do our reminiscing in private; it is unfair to ask others to listen to thousand-year-old anecdotes. And so it was one day as we drove along the rocky Mendocino coastline in northern California. We had discussed and decided against expanding the portion about the English doctor. The only exciting part of the doctor's life had been covered in a couple of paragraphs; to make any of the rest of it interesting would have required an elaborate embroidery. After a quarter hour of silence, Keetoowah said, "I was your father."

"You were what?"

"Your father. The Welsh coal mine owner." He then indicated where I should turn to take a primitive road which would get us home a half hour earlier, remarking that he'd seen a bear on this road just a year before. The coal miner had been dealt with.

I chewed on that one for a long time. Oh, I remember my father in 19th century Wales and even have a shadowy impression of my mother who died when I was in my early teens. But a curtain closes after I form an image of a heavy, bearded man who ritually drank a tumbler of peat-filtered whiskey before blessing the food at breakfast. I could not, and cannot to this day equate the cold man I constantly feared with the gentle, abstemious friend who rode beside me and asked me to stop the car so he could watch squirrels at play. When Keetoowah takes the leisure to turn his mind back to Victorian Britain, then perhaps I shall come to know the man who fathered me over a century ago.

If called upon to summarize the account of this next lifetime, I suppose I *would have to call it a little story about a couple of little lives and let it go at that. I am not sure I even like the overbearing, weak-willed Abdul but there's something sadly appealing about his bumbling. I loved Scherenome from the outset, initially because her name has such a musical lilt to it. . . Sher-ah-no-me. Then, of course, there is the aura of feral fascination which surrounds any untamed and untamable creature. Lastly, there is the recognition of character traits which appeared time after time, weaknesses which were doubtless a strong motivation in us, between lives, to attempt to correct.*

"Descendent of a dog!" The huge Salazhir bellowed and caught the boy when he had run no more than three steps from the doorway. How in the name of all that's holy, Abdul wondered for the hundredth time, can a man that size move so fast? "I'll fix your ears so you'll not eavesdrop again," Salazhir said and cuffed the boy on the side of the head with a hardened, cupped hand. Abdul fell, skidded and with one fluid motion was up and running. Knowing the Turk would not follow, Abdul trotted across the open garden space separating the master's house from the kitchen building, a long, narrow structure above and fifty yards behind the main house.

Pausing outside the kitchen to listen for his mother, the only person whom he really feared, Abdul climbed the embankment behind the kitchen until he was under the hand-hewn, square stone aqueduct which brought water from the artesian pool nearly a mile away. He loosened a slate which was inserted to divert the water to other channels. The cool water leaked out in a steady trickle and he put his head under it, pushing his long hair up to catch and absorb the coolness. His ear was beginning to throb and he knew, if he didn't learn to get out of the Turk's way quicker, that one day the man would rupture his eardrums with one of his blows.

He understood Salazhir's frustration at being relegated to what he considered a minor post in favor of a half-grown boy, and he felt no enmity for the big man who had been his master's companion and bodyguard since childhood. He only wished the master would be more firm; it was the master himself who had told Abdul to always be within call, which was why the lad squatted, nomad-fashion, outside the doorway, only half-listening to the conversation within. Listening, yes, but eavesdropping!!! Abdul sniggered and blew water from his nose. If he wanted information, including what went on in the master's bedroom, he needed only to bluster and threaten one of the two dozen cowering servant girls and get it. Provided he could get around his mother. He stirred uneasily, replaced the slate in the aqueduct and began to fluff his hair in the sun to dry it. His mother didn't beat him. . . it would be better if she did. His mother would only stare into his eyes until he had to look away and say, "One doesn't become strong by preying on weakness."

Seeing the master walking with Salazhir toward the stables which were removed from the main living compound and built where the water from the aqueduct could sluice through the building and on down the hillside, Abdul knew he would not be called there. "Abdul is a house man, not a horse man," the master had mildly rebuked the Turk when Salazhir had sought to punish Abdul with a stint of cleaning the stables. This was true. Abdul feared and hated horses, a well-remembered feeling dating from the time when, with childish bravado designed to impress Scherenome, he had tried to mount the master's great white stallion and the beast had bared his yellow teeth and earnestly tried to bite Abdul's leg off just below the knee. The ridicule from the other servants had been harder to bear than the pain during the weeks it took the leg to mend.

Recalling that he had been told to unpack and expose to the sun the tents and clothing the master would take on his trip, Abdul returned to the main house, turning his mind to the overheard conversation which had infuriated Salazhir. "I don't like it!" The Turk's voice seemed to bellow even in conversation. "Leaving that arrogant young whelp in charge on counting day."

"But I need you for this journey." The master's voice was calm, reasonable. "Only you can take us through the pass dominated by your bandit kinsmen."

"Turks they are. Kinsmen they are not," Salazhir rumbled, but his voice was pleased. "I just don't like that pup Abdul having this much authority."

"The choice is not yours, nor is it mine. The lad is the only member of the household who can read and write. . . even in the language of the English."

"That was money ill spent, sending him to study with those foreign thieves."

"You shall see, Salazhir. The boy will be the best steward we've ever had. He has a quick mind and is a wonder with counting, using the system he learned from your hated English. Be tolerant, old friend. Remember, you never even learned your letters."

"There was no need for that in the days of real men." The Turk was defensive now. The conversation would soon end. "I only wish we had a real man to leave behind."

Abdul could feel the smile in the master's voice. "He is man enough to blow up the belly of his cousin."

"There is much talk of that, even in the stables," Salazhir said.

"Yes, I know. I wish they could marry. I shall have to do something about that on our return."

Abdul repeated that last remembered sentence over and over in his head as he tugged the heavy tent sections out onto the wide stone porch. It would never occur to him to approach the master with a direct question. Such a thing was done only with caution even by Salazhir. But he felt a vague twinge of fear and thought to call Scherenome to talk about it. He continued with his work, though, hearing her voice in a far part of the house, singing a song in the strange language of the hill people. She should not by rights be working at cleaning the master's house in her condition. She should be away, with the other women, being instructed in how to care for the new life in her belly, how to bring it to the light of day with dignity and peace. But it was not even spoken of openly that she was with child. . . except in the stables, Abdul thought bitterly. How could she be with child when she had no husband? And how could she have a husband when the only man she had lain with was her cousin, the son of her mother's sister?

Abdul knew the blood was too heavy between them to speak of marriage, especially not in the household of a mighty prince, although it was said the peasants who worked the land paid little heed to such things. Scherenome, with eyes as dark and wild as the winter winds coming down from the hills, had told him this. Scherenome, rebellious, frightened and hungry, who might have starved crouched in a darkened corner of the kitchen had not Abdul come to her late at night with food from his own plate which she devoured . . . but not before biting him viciously in the hand. He had taken her with him to the storehouse where he worked and slept. There, with the uncluttered wisdom of childhood, he taught her love and the security of serving a kind and generous master. This was Scherenome, who had scarcely cast a shadow when his mother had brought her to the house as a trembling eight-year-old and said, "This is my sister's child."

With a practiced eye on his work, Abdul found a silken pillow which was mildewed and torn at one corner. He knew the master would no longer want it but debated about keeping it himself. Scherenome could turn the mildewed side down and repair the corner with her quick clever fingers but his mind hesitated when he visualized how conspicuous the bright richness would be in the plain little room they shared. On the other hand, if he returned it to the tentmaker, the tentmaker would surely sell it for his own profit. He put the pillow aside. Scherenome would have an answer.

He knew she would keep the pillow but it was easier to have someone else make a firm decision, although some of her answers often confused him and left him silent for long hours. In the early years, when they had held each other for warmth in the musty sweetness of the granary, she would tell him of her life in the hills. She spoke of the strange powers and knowledge of the people she called the oracles. . . men and sometimes women who know your thoughts, your past and future. It was an oracle she had visited soon before coming to the house who had told her she would return to the hills. She would cry then and say, "I don't want to return to the hills. It's a hungry land."

As her weeping quieted, she would try to tell him of the oracle. "He is not a fearsome man," she would explain when Abdul would swear great threats against an old man safely in the hills. "But if he caused you unhappiness he should die for it," Abdul would mutter. She would protest again and then fall silent when she could find no words to describe the childhood scene still etched as if in slate on her memory.

She had attempted to creep nearer to the poor fire one bitter night too cold for sleep when her family huddled in a grumbling mass and swore at the mother who fed the fire with miserly handfuls of twigs. Scherenome tried to edge a skinny shoulder between two almost-grown brothers and they both cuffed her viciously. Thus aroused, they fought while Scherenome lay in terror where she had fallen near the door, tasting the blood in her mouth while her legs became numb from the icy wind whipping around the tattered, stinking sheet of felt hung in the door frame. The mother and father kicked the boys into docility but neither came to see Scherenome. "That child is becoming more troublesome," the father said.

"Aye," the mother said. "She does little but whine for food and complain of the cold."

"We should have taken her out and exposed her at birth."

"It was summer then, you fool," the mother snarled at him. "The oracle would have found her and returned her to us under threat of a spell. Besides, you were the one who doted on her as a baby and assured me she would take all labor from my hands--and before now!"

Scherenome had dozed during this familiar argument but came rigidly awake at her father's words, " . . aye, well, then. I will take her out when we take the pelts to sell." So she was to be exposed, after all, taken into the frozen mountains, stripped and left to die! She did not know of any family which had done this, but she had heard the tales and believed them, and an older boy had once brought down a fragment of what could have been the skull of a human infant. Heedless of any consequence now, she quietly took her mother's shawl and wrapped it around her body. She tore strips from her own ragged dress to wrap around her feet, slipped out the door and stumbled with desperate haste toward the oracle's hut across the valley.

When she fell and could not rise again, she knew it was the oracle who lifted her and carried her on. Although she had never seen him, a comfortable mustiness of age and wood smoke came from his rough clothes and she felt a security she had not yet known. He laid her before a small bright fire in his hut and gave her a strangely seasoned bread which, although alien to her tongue, she devoured. She slept.

She awoke as a wild thing, knowing exactly where she was and in instant fear that her mother would soon be on her in a screaming rage for the theft of the shawl. The oracle put bread on the floor before her but she did not touch it until he had withdrawn. He did not speak until she had eaten. "You are safe here," he said. "They fear me too much to come for you. Rest and share my bread. Tomorrow I will take you back."

"NO!" The sound rushed from her with all the force of her body. "NO!"

The oracle laughed, and the opening of his toothless mouth gave a sudden warm mobility to the ancient face. His flesh was still firm under the lined and dusty-looking skin. His pate was bald; whitish hair began below the crown of his head and fell in wispy straggles to his shoulders. She did not have the words, even for her own mind, but she did not fear him. "Tell me, child," he said gently. "When you share fear with the one who has no fear, you have destroyed it."

In brief sentences, she told him what had happened the night before. Warm and with her belly full for the first time in her memory, she wanted to tell him it was true, what he said, that she was no longer afraid. Not very much. But she did not say that, recalling that he had said he would take her back in the morning.

"Yes, I will take you back," he said, and she stared at him, wondering how he could answer a question that was only in her mind. "Your parents mean only to take you out of the hills, not to kill you." He held out his hand as she scrambled to her knees as if to run. "Stay. Your mother has a sister who left the hills as a young girl. She went with a man who was a trader in furs. He was a good man and kept her with him until she was heavy with his child and could no longer travel. Then he gave her to a rich man who lives beyond the mountains, a merchant prince who is a buyer of furs."

Scherenome stirred with interest. "Did she become a harem girl?" she asked, although she had only a faint idea what the term meant.

The oracle frowned. "No. She was of the hill people which means she did not have an empty head. Word has come back that she now holds a place of importance in a great house. It is surely to your mother's sister that she will send you."

Scherenome sat for a long time, thinking about it. She stretched her imagination to its limits and finally asked a question which made her blush and bite her lip, because she knew it was purest fantasy. "Will there always be enough to eat?" The oracle nodded. She did not believe him. "Even in winter?" He nodded again and she stared at him, holding him with her dark eyes while her hand crept slyly over the floor to snatch a bread crust he had left on a clean board by his side.

The oracle leaned forward to tend the fire so he would not have to watch her wolf the bread. "But later, child, you will return to the hills," he said. Her mouth crammed with bread, she shook her head violently. He stared long into the fire. "Yes, you will return. I will await you here to give what comfort I can. I will also be with you from time to time. You need but to ask and I will answer."

She remembered, and sometimes when wild urgings tore like tempests at her being, she called to the oracle and he soothed her. Later, when Abdul's leg swelled and darkened after the horse had bitten him, the oracle sent her to the fields for herbs which she boiled to a pulp and used as a poultice, fiercely protecting him and defying even his mother.

Abdul could not comprehend when she tried to explain, and rather than make the effort, pulled his own meager thoughts around him, as he did now while brooding over the master's words to Salazhir. 'I shall have to do something about that,' the master had said. But what. . .? Abdul wanted to claw at the thickness in his skull with his fingers. He could not turn them out, this was their home. The master had taken troublesome servants and given them to other masters but they always had another home. If they were too troublesome, of course, he would have Salazhir kill them and be done with it. At sixteen, Abdul was a man of the world, he had traveled far and learned much, but he could not grasp this problem. It did not enter his mind there could be life without Scherenome as part of it, a part of him.

Was it not Scherenome who at the risk of grave punishment

had traveled two days to meet him when he returned last year after his two years with the English in the trading settlement they had built on the great sea? How had she known when he was coming. . . the road he would take? She only said her oracle came to her and told her during a dream, but this was the babble of a kitchen maid and Abdul would not listen. There had been no such talk by the sea where there were many great English houses and ships greater than houses which came out of nothingness over the horizon.

Abdul had felt an exciting stirring in his groin when he crested the last great hill at the end of the mountains and saw that the lone figure he had watched throughout the morning was Scherenome. With a grand gesture, he sent back the man to whom he had given gold to guide him through the mountains. After they had eaten the food she had brought and warmed themselves against the evening's chill by the fire he had struck, he lay with on his saddle blanket and attempted to take her. She lay unmoving, her dark eyes searching his face. "I don't think I can yet," she said, holding herself with one hand and indicating her newly-developed breasts with the other. "Besides, you've hurt me."

"It always hurts the first time. I know how." And he did, as much as an adolescent boy can learn during his farewell party when the clerks he worked with bought wine and took him to a caravan filled with filthy blankets and the smell of oil lamps and stale perfume. The young girl who spoke a strange language had not wanted to take him because his skin was dark, but his companions gave her more silver, and wine from their leather bags. She would not let them watch and kept the boy-man Abdul with her the night, marveling at his virility and cradling his head while he slept. She wept drunkenly at his lost innocence and never during her brief life gave thought to the fact that they were exactly the same age.

Abdul's training in the English trading center on the sea was put to the test when he returned to the house. Scherenome sat silent and motionless, where she could see Abdul's face, when he sat with the crotchety old steward on counting-day. Abdul would make swift, sure calculations and make notations on the rough skin-textured paper he had persuaded the master to buy at great cost from the English. The steward, who could not understand the strange writing which moved from the left to the right of the page instead of the normal right to left, gave over the record-keeping to the young man, reserving the privilege of his station, that of doling out the hardwood talents with the inscription of the house burned into them. These tokens, about two by six inches with a hole burned in one end so they could be strung on a rope, would be redeemed during the bitter winter for grain, precious metal farm implements or, if one could accumulate enough of them, a horse. In exchange for the talents, the peasants brought bales of homespun linen and wool and woven and delicately dyed carpets which would grace Western palaces for a century without showing wear. Since the opening of Western trade on the Caspian Sea a half century before, the peasants had never known such prosperity.

The old steward froze to death one night when he fell while checking the earth-and-straw packing heaped on the precious aqueduct to keep the water from freezing. Fearfully, Abdul went to the master's house when summoned, feeling he was somehow responsible for the old man's death. "You are yet too young to be steward," the master said. "You will continue to keep the records and sit with me on counting-days until I feel you are ready. For the sake of convenience, you will stay in the house."

Stunned but happy, Abdul returned to the granary and Scherenome. "We are to live in the house." If the master was surprised to see Abdul return hand in hand with Scherenome, he gave no indication. He, in fact, moved his favorite concubine back to the harem rooms and gave Abdul her room instead of a pallet on the floor as he had planned. Scherenome laughed and cried as she paced the confines of the room which represented the most luxurious privacy she had ever dreamed of. "But, Abdul, are you sure the master told you to bring me?"

Abdul shrugged. "He did not say NOT to bring you. Everyone knows we belong to each other."

When Scherenome learned she was with child, she went first to Abdul's mother, who ruled the kitchen with an uncompromising discipline. "Why do you come to me?" the woman said. "You are my sister's child. You cannot marry Abdul. Not in this house."

"But as my mother's sister, you can show mercy," the girl wept.

"There is no room in a harsh life for pity for doomed fools."

"But what will happen to me?"

"Abdul will send you away."

"He won't! He can't! We're part of each other!"

"He will send you away."

"If I have to go, he will go with me." She swept her skirts and made the fire under the nearest oven flare and spark. "If we are doomed fools, we'll be doomed together."

"So be it," the older woman said, but the girl was gone. Abdul's mother sat long by her stoves that night, until the fires were cold and dead.

Scherenome went with Abdul to clear the aqueduct before the onset of winter. This was the steward's most critical responsibility, to assure a constant supply of water to the house. The pool had never failed, even spilling its waters over its sides in the dreadful heat of midsummer, but the upper few feet froze solid during the fierce winters. Someone, before the memory of anyone then living, had tunneled deep through the stone to tap the pool below its freezing level. To prevent clogging, a screen of laced green willows was kept in place before the opening. This screen had to be replaced each winter before the freeze and Abdul now stood trying to remember the exact location so he would only need to make one descent into the icy water. "When we have a forge, I will make an iron screen that will never need to be replaced," he said, and stepped into the water with the new screen hooked over his arm. He waded, neck-deep, until he found the opening, then sank into the water. The job was not easy and he was blue with cold when he finally stood naked with Scherenome rubbing him warm with his robe.

"Abdul, I'm going to have a child."

He pulled the robe from her and held it before him, as if suddenly conscious of his nakedness. "What do you mean you're going to have a child? You can't have a baby. You're only sixteen."

"I was only fifteen when you raped me."

"I didn't rape you. You helped. But you're not REALLY going to have a baby, are you?"

"Yes."

He said nothing more as they went back down the hillside to the house. She now knew these silences meant he was trying to push unpleasant thoughts from his mind, and he usually succeeded. They sat to rest in his favorite secluded place behind the kitchen. She took his hand and gently passed it back and forth on her abdomen. "You can already feel it a little."

He sighed. "This is really good. You know, to have children so early. We will have a large family to work for us before we are even old."

"But we can't marry, Abdul. We're cousins."

"What difference does that make? Everybody knows we can't marry."

"Your mother says you have to send me away."

"That old hag is always meddling in my affairs," he said, but he could not keep from lowering his voice and glancing at the window-less back wall of the kitchen building. He tried to swear a blasphemous oath he had learned from the English-by-the-sea but could not remember all the words.

Thereafter Scherenome seldom left the house except to empty and scour the enameled earthenware chamber pots down behind the stables, or to walk across the courtyard at dusk to the drab harem quarters to fetch a companion when the master did not want to be alone. When she learned the master was leaving to negotiate with the English traders when the snow was gone from the passes, she began to sing again. Abdul smiled and held her close when he returned from riding the obligatory half day with his master as he left with his caravan. "Ah, it's good for a woman to be happy when her man is placed in charge of a great household. I am in truth the steward now. The counting is next week and I will do well."

"I am very proud," she said softly. "But I am most happy because the master will be gone for six weeks, maybe more. And my time is soon."

"Not this soon," he said, looking down at her body.

"But look how big I am. We must have made a mistake in the reckoning. I am happy because now it will happen while the master is gone. I will move to the harem. The fair-haired girl who claims to be part English has said she will help me. I have been kind to them and they like me." She loosened the thongs of his riding tunic and rubbed his chest. "They will keep the baby in the harem with the other babies and by the time the master returns all will be forgotten." In point of fact, this was almost precisely what the master had in mind. He valued Abdul's plodding efficiency, knowing the boy was bright enough to develop into an excellent steward yet dull enough to be completely loyal, never daring to presume beyond the privileges which would be his as steward. The master was more attuned to the gossip of his servants than his outer indifference indicated, and his half-formed resolution to effect a change in the pregnant Scherenome's living status was only a mild desire to make life more tolerable for the girl.

Abdul said nothing while he ate and then bathed and dried his hair, saddled with the unfair burden of his own thoughts. It was only after Scherenome slept that he awakened her and told her what the master had said to Salazhir.

"I don't understand," she said. "What does he mean, 'do something about it'? There will be nothing left to do. He has never set foot in the harem and won't know one baby from another. Only we will know, when we take it out when the master is gone."

Abdul took a deep breath and began one of the longest speeches of his life. "You have never traveled, so it is you who do not understand. Our master is a great merchant prince. When he returns he will have with him other princes and their caravans and servants. He has told me to prepare for them. There is much talk among the servants here about what has happened between us, even the stable people talk of it."

She tossed her head. "I hear enough from those stable people every morning."

"Then you do understand! We cannot have a moral disgrace right within the master's family, as it were."

"You're not family. You're just the storehouse keeper."

"I'm the steward. And if I'm not family, why am I honored by living under the same roof with the master?" He hugged himself and turned away from her. "Anyway, what would be our master's reputation if. . . all this became known among the other princes?"

Her voice was very quiet and without expression. "Then you are sending me away."

"Don't say it that way. It's just that it will be better if you are not here when the master returns."

"Where shall I go?"

"You can visit your mother for a few weeks. You haven't seen her since you came here."

"My mother's village is two days' horseback ride into the hills. She gave me away because there was not enough food. I do not even know if she is still alive."

"Ah, I will send a horse with you. . . and food." He stretched and yawned. "Anyway, there's nothing to worry about. No need to even think about it for another month."

But when he awoke in the morning, she was gone.

———————⇒ ⇐———————

The way to the hills was long and even now, in the second season, the times after sundown were frigid and filled with wind. Scherenome spent the first night huddled, sleepless, against the horse she had stolen. As the quick sharpening of the wind told of another night at hand, she tied the horse to a twisted tree and resolved to master the strange fire-maker Abdul had brought from the English-by-the-sea. The four-inch slab of flint fitted into a worn wooden frame was deeply grooved in the center, obviously from the finger-sized, rounded piece of iron which was wedged into the frame. Doubting, she stroked the iron down the flint and cried out with delight when it was followed by a shower of sparks. . . so much easier than pounding two black stones together over dried moss for fire!

Not consciously aware that she had reverted instantly to the generations of habit of the hill people, Scherenome mixed rancid goat's milk with rough-ground flour and worked it into a round, flat cake. This she plastered on a flat rock which she set at an angle to the fire. She browned it on one side, then the other, catching it and deftly juggling it to cool when it began to slide off the rock. She ate slowly, thinking only that this was the last of the goat's milk. But she had a goodly supply of the flour. She hadn't meant to take so much, it had been an effort to get it on the horse, but it was the only bag she could find and although they would grumble, the kitchen maids would grind out a new supply today.

When she thought of the kitchen she thought of Abdul's mother and the gloomy prophecy. It was not a thing to toss to the winds, a prophecy. Although Abdul's mother had been in the prince's house since she was a young girl, she was nevertheless one of the hill people. Restless, Scherenome got up and tried to urge the reluctant horse nearer to share the fire with her. "Ah, horse, don't fear the fire. It is the only friend we have." Feeling less lonely with the sound of her own voice, she talked to the horse. "You must remember the trail well, horse, because you must find your way home alone. If my people are still in the village, they will eat you for sure. Even though it is foolishness not to keep you. Did not Abdul say he would send a horse when he sent me away?"

She gathered dried brush and when she had a heap as high as the horse's head, she shoved it into the fire. The inferno would warm the walls of the protected niche she had found and, sheltered from the wind, would keep her comfortable until morning. While waiting for the fire to die, she led the horse to a sparse pasturage she had seen earlier.

Scherenome spent yet another night before following the turbulent little stream through the deep defile to the valley where her home village lay. Two gaunt men rose from the sides of the path ahead and waited for her. "We are your brothers," one said. "I know" she answered, and followed them to the strongly built stone hut which appeared smaller than her memories of it. "My mother still lives?" she said. "She lives." "And my father?" Her brothers held the horse but did not help her dismount. "He went to the passes," one said. She understood. Hill people, when driven by hunger and privation, sometimes went to the passes to intercept and rob the merchants. They were inept at this and usually bungled the job but were most often slain by the professional Turkish bandits from the North.

"We will have bread today!" Scherenome's mother shrieked, and this was her only greeting. Scherenome said nothing as her mother dragged the big bag of coarsely ground flour into the hut, regretting only briefly that she had planned a month of frugal meals from this grain. There followed a day of baking, eating the bread half-cooked, vomiting it up and returning for more. Scherenome did not set the horse free that day. She took the remnants of the flour and used it as a pillow that night when the strongest of her brothers grudgingly relinquished his pad by the fireplace for her. While a cold crescent moon still cast a feeble light over the valley, she took the last of the grain and led the horse to the oracle's hut, two hours away at the foot of the next ridge of hills.

"You are late," the old man said, not turning around when she parted the tattered woolen door covering and entered to see the oracle rocking on his heels before a small hot fire.

She squatted beside him, then sat when her bulk overbalanced her. "How do you keep your fires so hot?"

"I follow woodcutters, dig up the roots of fallen trees and dry them."

"That is much work." She put the flour bag conspicuously between them.

"It is less work. My fires burn hotter and last longer." He reached out and hefted the flour. "Bake the bread tonight. To-morrow we will kill the horse."

"We can't kill the horse. It belongs to my master and he will make Abdul pay dearly for it." She got up to get the stone bowl in which she would mix the flour into dough. "Besides, the bread will spoil."

"The bread will not spoil when you mix this powder with it." He reached a skinny arm to hand her a covered wooden bowl. "God is your only master and God will not begrudge you a tired old horse. Bake the bread, child. Tomorrow I will show you how to cook and dry the meat of the horse. You will need the strength to suckle your babies."

"What do you mean, babies? The general order is to have one at a time."

"You will never abide by the general order, Scherenome. You will have two."

"Two? But I don't want any, not now."

"You will have two, when the moon changes again. And you will have them here. Bake the bread. I will talk to you until the sun rises, and then I must sleep." The old man talked until the dark turned to gray and then to light. He talked not of death but of life, the life she had brought to this world from lives of great strangeness lived beyond the darkness of the dimmest star. Of lives when this world was much younger and stronger and destroyed itself through the arrogance of this strength. When she was very tired and the bread was finished and lay cooling on blackened wooden shelves above the fireplace, she asked him about Abdul.

"Abdul is your mate. Look into the fire and begin to count the times he has been with you." The old man stretched and walked outside to relieve himself. And she saw. "But I still see him with me," she said when the old man returned. Yes, he explained, Abdul will come to you because no power on earth can keep him from you. "But then he must die with me," she wailed. "We are truly doomed fools, as his mother said."

"You cannot call one a fool who knows his own destiny and comes to meet it. Search the fire again. Therein you will find both cause and effect of your presence on this plane. Now, let me sleep." She stared into the embers until she slept, and in her dreams Abdul came to her, as she now believed he must.

———————

Abdul made a shambles of the counting-day and many peasants squatted, grumbling in the courtyard, until sundown. He worked many days trying to bring order to the records, but with each beginning the figures were strange and unfamiliar. Every evening before sunset he climbed to where he could see the trail he knew Scherenome had taken, straining his eyes with hope that finally became despair. One day, without thought or plan, he packed food into a blanket which he tied over his shoulders and walked into the hills, marvelling at the peace that now stroked his mind with gentle fingers.

He walked throughout the night, not hesitating when the main trail branched into a smaller one and yet another. His body told him when it must rest and eat. At the end of the third day Scherenome met him a mile from the oracle's hut and they went the rest of the way together, their arms around each other, not speaking. He slept the night with his head cradled in her lap. He awoke, ate and walked with Scherenome into the scraggly forest. She soon tired so they lay on the earth in the warmth of the sun and slept again.

That night they talked with the oracle, their hearts pounding with the slow tempo of the old man's words. Their minds grew and probed tentatively into expanding awareness. Joy filled them as the night wore away and when the old man rolled over and began to snore, they embraced, without touching, in the timeless, soft sweetness they had known for so long, and would know forever.

———————

There had been no food for three days when the babies, identical girls, were born. She held them to her dry breasts for a day and a night. Abdul was rubbing his finger softly on her cheek when her eyes widened and a gout of blood rushed from her. The babies whimpered but he took time to press her eyes closed before wrapping the infants and placing them near the warmth of the fire.

"What do we do with the babies, old man?" Abdul said when he had buried Scherenome.

"They will join her soon."

"Do you mean we just let them starve?"

"Do we have a choice?" The old man sighed. "In this country it will be a kindness."

"Then I must starve too."

"Yes, you will starve."

Abdul looked closely at the old man and spoke with more curiosity than malice. "And you, old one, I suppose you will live on?"

"I will live on. My body does not really require food."

Abdul spat on him with weary anger. "Why should you live forever and we die before we are grown?"

"I will not live forever. I know the time. It is not yet."

"You know everything, don't you?"

The old man laughed, a rare sound. "If I did, then there would be no reason to continue living."

Tired and not interested in continuing the argument, Abdul turned again to the pinched-faced babies. "I could take them to the harem girls. . ." He broke off and looked at his hands, still trembling violently from the exertion of digging the grave. He put his hands to his face and wept until he retched. "There is nothing left," he moaned.

"Everything is left," the oracle said. "You are more fortunate than most. You have found each other and learned the folly of acting without responsibility. Your Scherenome lives. Call her and she will be with you in the little time before you join her."

Abdul stared at the oracle with hatred in his eyes and rolled over on the floor, hugging his knees to his chest. But the misery that would have brought the relief of more tears did not come. He was conscious only of the dull hunger ache in his stomach.

Then the wonder began to spread in him. . .

. . . and he called his Scherenome. . .

. . .and she came.

In order to find material for a suitable epitaph for Abdul and Schere-nome I consulted a lady whose psychic sensitivities I respect. I outlined the story, the situation, and asked if any impressions of the oracle appeared. I was eager to learn this; an elusive memory has long flickered on and off as the images of those final weeks with the oracle try to focus themselves. I recorded no conversations but still retain thought forms from then which reveal more than we previously knew about our forms and status during our lives-between-lives. There are shadows which momentarily clear to reveal brilliant, almost frightening fragments of awareness of life as it is in expanded areas of consciousness.

The lady I visited had met Keetoowah, but only casually at various local functions. She gave me a sharp look and said, "The oracle was Keetoowah. His physical appearance hasn't changed much. He seems to have used a mild, benevolent mind control on the two of you. Wait. . . you were two of ten whose minds were guided by the oracle. There were always ten, and he had a long life. Somehow, he tuned in and attracted old, experienced souls in-habiting mortal bodies. Hmm. This is unusual. He was 100 years old when you came to him to die. Then he lived another century." I interrupted to re-mind her that there are eastern holy men who have, according to convincing evidence, lived several hundreds of years in physical form and for whom con-tinued longevity is a matter of choice. She shook her head and told me the oracle was not of this genre, although he had attained sufficient mastery over his body to require little or no food. He had apparently chosen an earthly incarnation and brought with him full knowledge of what he was doing. Several members of his celestial family were, in a manner of speaking, doing time on this earthly plane in the same general geographical area during that period and Keetoowah had joined them as a sort of spiritual father figure.

I cannot actively espouse this account because it isn't in my conscious memory. Nor, oddly, can Keetoowah. He is emphatic that he was indeed the oracle and can recall enough to tie us to Abdul and Scherenome but the more ethereal aspects are lost to him. Anything further would be pure speculation, although it is tempting to visualize trance states, partial posses-sion by collective or individual oversouls, or even try to unsnarl some conflicting thoughts on elementals.

But this would be supposition, not a factual reporting of personalized history. We will do better to send belated blessings with the pathetic young-sters as they found relief and peace in physical death. It was a good transition and the chance to view again those short lives has been instructive to us both.

IV

Communication with the spirit world becomes far more rewarding when you realize that you're talking to people just like yourself, people who can show worry, irritation and on rare occasions, jealousy. They have access to vastly more information of every nature than we do, but they confess to making mistakes, they are capable of pulling the leg of the gullible with fantastic yarns and many who have not attained a high level of development can be downright naughty, giving misleading information or impersonating some friend or relative. Many spirit impersonators are not content with anything less than the grandiose, presenting themselves in all solemnity as anyone from Alexander the Great to Marie Antoinette to Winston Churchill. Unfortunately, these imposters are believed by many sincere but sadly equipped (spiritually) people. We deplore this, as do our friends in spirit who work so valiantly to help those of us on this mortal plane.

The most endearing, HUMAN trait of our spirit friends is their earthiness and full-bodied sense of humor. During the weeks we were transcribing the notes from the Poet on past lifetimes, we would end each session with general light conversation. One evening we were being regaled by a spirit character who identified himself as Popo and by his description of his attire we placed him as one of the fanciest of the dandies of around 1920. When asked what he had done for a living he replied that he was a 'tomato sorter'. Oh, Carol said, you worked in a canning factory. No, Popo hadn't worked in a canning factory. His 'tomatos' were the ones he'd ogled while they were taking their Sunday afternoon strolls. I remarked that he sounded like a Damon Runyon character and he replied that Runyon was there and did I want to talk to him.

The nature of the communication changed to where I knew another personality was there. The new entity identified himself as Runyon and we chatted about some of his writings. He then commented on my writings and said I would become the 'Damon Runyon of psychic writers'. I responded that I would prefer to be known as the Harry Green of psychic writers. Now, I have no idea whether I really talked with the spirit of Damon Runyon or not but that isn't important. Whoever it was had wit and humor and made it a fun experience.

I hesitate to put a number to the many sittings, readings, seances, etc. in which I have participated. The greater majority of these had at least a token religious overtone, many included hymn singing and prayer. I like this because, as I have earlier stated, the investigation of the world of the spirit is of genuine religious significance to us. Until I became adept enough to do my own communicating, I often wondered at the stilted, formal nature of the communicators themselves which often inhibit the frequent natural exuberance of the spirits. The mediums have steeped themselves in a traditional format of ritual and will only give forth conversation which fits this format. The exception to this is the trance medium who, if taken over by a fun-loving 'control' can be highly enter-taining. Most trance mediums, though, if of a sedate nature seem to attract similar spirit controls.

The most amusing come-uppance I've had with a spirit was not in direct communication but while on an astral trip. I have been guided to a means whereby I can separate my astral from my physical body while conscious, but just barely. I can sometimes induce it when I am in physical pain; my astral is removed from my physical like a blurred photograph where the camera is moved but does not, consciously, go any further than is necessary to separate me from pain. I am frequently aware of astral travel, in detail, but do not control it. On this particular occasion I had spent considerable time attending a musical concert in a massive temple. As I left, I encountered Tom, a boyhood chum and lifelong friend who had passed over a few years before. Overjoyed, I ran to him, embraced him and wrung his hand. He accepted my enthusiastic affection kindly and patiently but without reciprocating enthusiasm. Not to be daunted, I bubbled on, 'Tom, old Tom! It's so great to see you. It's downright wonderful! Just to think, running into you like this! Why, why. . . I though you were dead!' At this last, he gave me a long look and said, 'What in the hell do you think I'm doing here?' With that, he waved casually and walked off. What indeed?

For pure, zestful, rollicking enjoyment of life, none can surpass the spirit of the Uncle, a personage I knew and loved dearly during his life on earth. As mildly as I can state it, the Uncle's earthside vocabulary was uninhibited. Alas, his passing on to spiritual form has not laundered his language a bit, although some claim it is redeemed by touches of poetry woven through the profanity. In life on earth, the Uncle was a man of temperate habits, except eating, and after his retirement he acquired an *impressive poundage. Talking to him in spirit, I twitted him about this and he replied with a very believable story of how he had modified his physical form to become slim, youthful and graceful. Our oldest daughter is a far more potent psychic than I am and not infrequently receives visible spirit manifestations. In relating one such visitation by a spirit unfamiliar to her, she described the Uncle, unmistakably. She was quite firm in her conviction that the spirit as it appeared to her was definitely 'portly'.*

I challenged him with this information and am sure the very atmosphere vibrated with his roar (he could always roar wondrously), "That's not fair!"

In the transcribing of the following lifetime we were still hung up on attempting to fix historical dates to our adventures. The Poet, our faithful scribe, became increasingly distressed as we insisted on dates and verifiable events and geographical locations. To help ensure that our own minds would not interfere with information we were receiving from the spirit realm, we did no research until the first draft of the book was completed. Subsequent research was made to satisfy our natural curiosity; no changes in the manuscript were made, even when it conflicted with such frowning authorities as the Encyclopedia Britannica.

For example, historians are in complacent agreement that the horse was introduced to the North American continent by the Spanish, at about the beginning of the 17th century. In our chronicle of White Mouse, however, the western American Indians had the horse at the first appearance of 'the strangers' who we are sure were the earliest Spanish explorers. Interestingly, a number of anthropologists also believe the horse existed in North America long before the Spaniards came. This proves nothing, of course, but it did add excitement to our after-the-fact investigations.

Back to the Poet, who tried repeatedly to explain to us that the concept of measurable time existed only on our present plane of existence. This form of the humanoid organism (man) was born, grew, aged and died. To account for these physiological changes, he separated the seasons and named them because they recurred with predictable frequency. It was then but a step into the evolution of mathematics leading to the measuring of lightness and dark and the ultimate division of these periods into miniscule fragments which, in turn, could be calculated by the accuracy of the earth's position in relation to the visible universe--the sun, moon, stars and constellations. To the Poet, it is possible that our earthly life form is the only one known which has made the attempt to reduce a particle of eternity to symbols identified by numbers. We figure the Poet's earthly body died long enough ago for him to absorb the concept of infinity which cannot be brought into focus by the human mind--and long enough to forget the ephemeral triviality of attempting to set physical, numerical limits to eternity, which has no limits in either direction.

In living again the lives of Okla and Portlona, the feeling we invariably had was Russian, as emphatically as I feel the Irish rising in me with the approach of Saint Patrick's Day. The 'city' around which the story is centered, however, was always given to us as Krakow. Even to one as culturally illiterate as myself, it is pretty generally accepted that Krakow is in Poland, not Russia. Yet, the impression of Russia persisted and perhaps someone with more scholarly inclinations will reveal that Krakow was once a part of Russia. I am compelled to make this disclaimer to placate the Poet, who has grudgingly assented to the substitution of 'the city' for what he is convinced really was the city of Krakow, and at some point in history a part of Russia.

We have now joined with the Poet in giving a resounding 'Pfaugh!' to all nit-pickers. It would doubtless involve difficulty, but I am confident the Poet could marshall exact names, dates and places. We are all in agreement, though, that I am not a good enough medium to report these things with any degree of dependability. It is penance enough, I think, to see myself through repeated lifetimes as a non-hero.

Barefoot peasants, their trousers legs pulled above their knees to escape the mire, were still spreading sawdust in the stable yard to absorb the mud and moisture from the previous night's rain when Okla and his father rode up. All work stopped and several men moved away when Okla's father wheeled his horse and made him rear. Fearful that his father would be recognized, even at this place, a day's ride from the city, Okla nevertheless felt admiration at the sight of his six and a half foot father on horseback. Although he no longer wore his hair in the military style, the old man was still a cavalryman, erect and in perfect control of the half-wild black stallion he had acquired in a questionable deal recently just for this occasion.

They dismounted and strode to the comfortable looking house almost hidden behind a small hill. "Do you own this farm, too, father?" Okla said, trying to match his father's stride.

"In partnership with your Uncle Teo," the man said absently. "Although our host has lived here all his life, as did his father before him."

Okla marveled, thinking of the half dozen or more farms, all owned by or owing allegiance to his father, which had been their temporary homes during the past two years while fleeing the czar's wrath in the city. He knew the family wealth was considerable, mostly with land acquired by past generations from other czars. Okla's forbearers had been military men as far as family history was recorded; they traditionally fought as mercernaries and took their payment in land, then settled their soldiers on this land. This was a prudent form of insurance, considering the capricious temperament of most czars of recent memory, although the advent of Christianity a century before had had at least a surface influence on the casual ruthlessness of those who named themselves czar over as much territory as they could govern.

Okla looked at the house and sighed. So this was where he was to celebrate his wedding day! The house was rooted with the solid assurance of permanance, constructed of stone and hewn, massive logs. Only a few weathered carvings graced the eaves. The lintel above the door was deeply carved but with a heavy rural hand, so unlike the sweeping designs on the house they had hurried from in the city late one night just two years ago. For Okla's wedding, this country house was decorated only with broad strips of dyed muslin draped over the door and hanging down each side of the door.

Okla waited outside until his father returned with the tenant, a man his father's age. Marriage to a girl he had never seen. . . and midst the stink of peasants! Okla made a wry face but then hung his head, thinking of the great risk his father was taking in having the wedding in the first place. This house, his father had explained, was chosen because a child had recently been born here and the festivities were to be combined with the christening in the event any of the czar's spies had ranged this far. The house was decorated for a country christening so the priest would have an excuse for being there; it was not decorated for the wedding of a son of a member of the czar's court. Uh. . .a former court member, Okla added to himself.

The wedding was to be that day because the priest did not dare stay overnight. Okla was hustled into the house, surrendered the ruffled lace shirt he was to wear so it could be freshened up and suffered the supreme indignity of being stripped of his trousers and boots by WOMEN so they could be cleaned of the stains from the morning's ride. Wrapped in a blanket, he sat in immobile humiliation, answering politely when his father came to spend a few minutes with him and offer him a cup of vodka, which he refused.

He unbent enough to ask his father details about Portlona, his bride-to-be, but his father either didn't know the girl or considered the whole thing unimportant. Okla knew only that Portlona was sixteen, the youngest of three daughters in a family of thirteen children, that she had been betrothed to him at birth by virtue of the lifelong friendship between his father and 'Uncle' Teo, an even more powerful member of the primitive military heirarchy. Uncle Teo was a grim, taciturn man, the antithesis of Okla's ribald, fun-loving father but when one considered that nine of Uncle Teo's sons had died in successive forays against the Balkan savages, this lack of vitality was understandable.

Okla knelt dream-like at the improvised altar, only partly aware of the stumbling Latin of the uneducated priest. The ceremony was ending and he still had not seen his bride, hidden as she was behind her veils. The priest leaned over and put his hand on Okla's shoulder. "Take your bride's hand, raise her and kiss her." His reverie broken by half-remembered instructions, Okla took the girl's hand and yanked her to her feet. He lifted her veil and paused with his hand in the air, numbed by the cold fury in the girl's almost-black eyes. He took a deep breath. So now I am married, he thought, to a witch who already hates me. Taking strength from his father who stood behind him, Okla put his other arm around his bride and said, for her only, "If you bite me, I will tear your ears off."

When the wedding was finished, Okla and Portlona were usher-ed to the rear of the room while the christening was done. Okla's father was "company-stage" drunk when this was done, and even Uncle Teo was embracing the peasants and the blushing wives. Embarrassed because he was unable to understand the peasant's dialect and because his new wife had disappeared to another part of the house, Okla took several gulping swigs from the pewter cup of home-brewed vodka when it came his way. Knowing he was going to be sick, he ran out of the house to the stable and was quietly retching when his father, now dressed as a farmer, came with a bag of provisions to get his horse. Okla wiped the sweat from his forehead with his sleeve. "What am I to do now, father?"

The giant soldier paused to focus his eyes on his son, then hugged him and lifted him from the ground. "Make children, my son, not conversation!" Suspecting that his son needed more de-tailed instructions on his wedding day, the father released the stallion to a stable hand and led his boy to the watering trough, where they sat together. "I cannot stay here, Okla. There are those in this party who will probably report this affair for the price of a spring lamb. As for you, go with your Uncle Teo to his house in the city. Live with him as a visiting relative. Oh ho! You will have your bride there, but until we figure something out, you must live under the shadow of your hunted father. I am very sorry about that, but you are my only son and upon you falls the burden of keeping the family blood flowing. Do well." The old soldier mounted his horse and, without a farewell salute, rode away, his body rigid in the saddle but canting a bit to the left as if to accommodate the sloshing of at least a liter of vodka.

Unsatisfied but cowed by years of obedience to his father, Okla stood until his father was out of sight, then found Uncle Teo. "Will you talk with me, Uncle Teo? I feel alone here in the country."

Uncle Teo took Okla's arm with a hand as brown and hard as carved oak. "We'll walk in the woods. The women make so much noise a man can't think." They walked for a quarter of an hour and Uncle Teo sat with his back to a tree, showing a soldier's indifference to the damp ground. Okla leaned against another tree, facing him. "I suppose you want to know about the bride your father and I have forced down your throat."

"I'll get to know her soon enough if I'm to live with her in your house," Okla said. "I really want to talk about my father. Is he in truth under sentence of death by the czar?"

To Okla's utter surprise, Uncle Teo roared with laughter. "Did he tell you that?"

"No, but we've been running and hiding for two years. . ."

"Your father is an incurable romantic, Okla. The worst that would happen to him at the hands of the czar would be to be stripped of his rank and turned out of the palace. Since he has left both his position and the palace, the only reason I've found for his chasing around like this is the sense of adventure it seems to give him. . . that plus a very natural desire to avoid a public disgrace."

"But what did he DO?"

"So he hasn't told you that, either? Small wonder. That could be another reason he's kept you out of the city, to keep you from finding out." Uncle Teo folded his hands behind his head and looked up into the tree. "I've just enough vodka in me to enjoy telling this story. As you know, your father was chief security officer in the palace guard company which is now commanded by my only living son." He paused and Okla could see his mind going back to the uncounted battles and nine dead sons somewhere in the South country. The man relaxed and smiled again. "The most important celebration of the year is the czarina's birthday. I think you were there once."

"Yes. When I was ten, I think."

"Well, most people enjoy celebrations but your father LOVES celebrations. Your father also loves the czarina with a true devotion. . . she's a good and gentle woman. . . and he intended no offense."

"But what did he DO?"

"He powdered his wig."

"My father put GUNPOWDER on his wig?"

"No, no, no. This is a white stuff with a sweet smell which I understand the women in France use on their bodies to hide the stink. . . and the men, too. One of the campaigners brought the czarina a quantity of it some years ago. She uses it for special holidays, and she's the only one in this protectorate allowed to use it, by royal mandate."

"But how did my father get it?"

"He stole it. . . how else? Your father, who has been known to celebrate the full moon, had been at the jug with some of the senior officers all night the day before the czarina's birthday. I don't know the details, but I shall never forget the sight of your father passing in review before the royal box with his black ceremonial wig powdered almost white. He was rigid as a statue and I'm sure I've never seen him more magnificently drunk." Uncle Teo pounded his thigh and laughed till the tears rolled down his face.

"And I'm supposed to stay in hiding the rest of my life just because my father got drunk on the czarina's birthday!"

"Don't make it sound so grim, Okla. My house is almost in the city and I doubt if any outcry would be made even if it were known who you are. I think it better this way, though, until your father makes peace with the czar."

Okla was only able to view his father in perspective when he was away from him. The older man's personality was so overwhelming that Okla was usually mute with awe and admiration, but he was also filled with an affection neither of them had learned to articulate. There were also memories of moments of exasperation which came up as a choking mixture of tears and laughter.

Uncle Teo's laughter had evoked a recollection of Okla's fourteenth birthday, a celebration which had been planned and executed with military flourishes and precision by his father. An impressive banquet was attended by boys Okla's age, sons of his father's fellow officers in the court. Young girls were of course excluded, in keeping with the contemporary illusion that the sexes didn't mingle until of marriageable age. The entertainment following the banquet, however, had more appeal for the all-male adult assemblage than for the youngsters, who were bundled hurriedly home on horseback so their fathers could return for dancing and serious drinking.

Accustomed to revelries in the great house, Okla went to his own apartment, sleepy after the heavy meal and a couple of glasses of wine. He had been long asleep when awakened by his father's boisterous roar in his bedroom. He looked up from his bed and shook his head violently to assure himself it was not a dream. His father stood in the center of the room, arms akimbo with a giggling dancing girl perched on each enormous shoulder. Each girl held a flaming torch which threw jerking, marionette shadows as she sought to maintain her balance. "Which shall it be!" the lusty Colonel roared. "Or can you manage them both?!" Entranced at the spectacle rather than the offer, Okla sat hugging his knees to his chest until the remnants of the party stormed into the room and dragged his father, still clinging to the girls, back to the ballroom.

This memory reminded him of the futility of trying to hold anger against his father, so he smiled to himself and asked, "What will that involve?"

"I expect an apology and quiet retirement from the palace guard will do it, but I suppose your father's right in letting the czar cool down another year or two. Some say the czar is afflicted with a kind of moon madness and the czarina is the only one who can control him when the sickness is upon him."

"But why wait?"

"I'd say the main reason is to get your house back. It's a valuable bit of property and we'd both like to see our grandchildren grow up there. But come, we must get back to the party while the vodka lasts."

They were within sight of the house when Okla spoke. "Are we to spend our wedding night HERE?"

Uncle Teo's voice was amused. "You have aristocratic tastes for a soldier's son. No, you'll start for the city in the coach as soon as you change clothes. You'll rest and change horses where you and your father stayed last night. We'll catch up with you tomorrow."

Okla did not recognize Portlona when she swept out of the house. She was slim where most Russian girls had begun to get thick. She wore trousers and a brightly patterned blouse under an ankle-length cape. She walked to him and said, "Are you ready?" When he said nothing, she handed him one of two blankets she carried and climbed into the carriage before he could move to help her. Waving half-heartedly to the people crowding out of the house, he followed her.

Seemingly from the impetus of her energy, the carriage began to move as soon as the door was closed. "Just the two of us?" he said. "What about your sisters?"

She curled her feet under her and faced him as he sat on the edge of the other seat. Her dark eyes held him until he felt the sweat under his arms. "Not only am I married against my wishes to a criminal, but he also turns out to be an idiot! What would people think if we returned as a family? With a new man along, they'd think we just returned from a wedding and the czar's men would be there within the hour to ask questions about your stupid father. Or don't you think at all?" He was still pondering his answer when they reached his new home in the city a day and a half later.

Uncle Teo's house was large. Two wings had been built onto the original house, forming a three-sided rectangle. One wing was closed and unused, the other had been renovated for the newly marrieds although their quarters were situated at the end, past the servant's quarters, to maintain the facade of the 'visiting relative.' The bedroom walls were covered with polished oaken slabs which gave an unintended intimacy to the huge room. A four poster bed of softly glowing cherry wood squatted massively on a large, round hooked rug which Portlona had unwillingly helped her sisters make. Half of an adjoining room had been partitioned to make a kitchen, the other half the dining and parlor area.

Their first night, tired from the trip, they ate cold meat and dark bread while servants heated water on the new iron stove which surely must have been brought from as far away as Warsaw at great cost. Portlona took several hot bricks wrapped in rags to the bed, then turned. "You'll want to bathe." Okla didn't want to bathe. He had bathed only the week before, but, glad to cover his embarrassment with activity, he undressed and sat in a large wooden tub in the kitchen while an old woman poured steaming water over him. He was delighted to find the outhouse just outside the long hall running the length of the house wing. Just a few steps away, the privy was connected to the house by a roofed and walled corridor. "It's new," the old woman said with quiet pride.

Okla settled into the soft feather mattress while Portlona bathed. She came to him wrapped in a floor-length garment of some unbleached material. She sat beside him with the coverlet pulled up to her chin. "You will find me a virgin," she said, her voice cool and controlled.

Okla, every vertebra aching from the long ride, almost huffing with pent-up frustration and humiliation, jerked his body up beside her. "I'll find you in hell, too," he shouted at his witch-child wife. "As far as I'm concerned you can remain a virgin throughout eternity, damn your ears!"

She shook her head until her dark hair fell like a sooty halo around her shoulders. She studied his face. "You do have a thing about my ears, don't you?" she said, then blew out the candle and lay down with her back to him.

Okla rode out the next morning, anxious to see the city after an absence of two years. He saw little change in the place which had been his home since birth; some buildings were being faced with the colorful titles from the new kilns by the river which sent the sweet smell of wood smoke over the city by day and cast a ruddy glow against the sky at night. Despite a gentle warning from Uncle Teo, Okla rode into the street where he had lived and found the street newly paved with granite blocks. This would please his father, who had complained of the quagmire always before their door during the rainy summers before the snows came.

His only friends had been boys his own age, boys of other military families who were probably doing their barracks time by now. Okla knew not to approach the barracks or the palace so he turned his horse to the street of the merchants. Here he selected material and was measured for new clothing. He directed the tailors to come to his new home for subsequent fittings. Taking a bemused detour through streets where he had raced his horse and played at being a soldier, he returned home.

In his own apartment he found Portlona at the stove, the dining table neatly set for two. "You can cook," he said, surprised.

She didn't turn. "It is a wife's duty to care for her husband's needs."

He pulled a chair to where he could watch her and sat backwards on it, his arms resting on the back. "I know little of such things. I never knew my mother."

"That's right. She died when you were born. Who cooked for you?"

He shrugged. "Servants when there were guests. Mostly I ate with friends or with my father in one of the inns in the city."

She looked at him with a kindling interest, appreciating for the first time his dark good looks, muscular body and good posture from his military upbringing. He had a mobile face, quick to smile, and she had a momentary feeling of familiarity, as though she had known him for long although she had never seen him before the wedding. She almost yielded to an impulse to go to him and touch him. But then the willful childishness in her arose as she thought of the splendid wedding she could have had instead of the hurried secret affair far from civilization. She served him, almost throwing the food onto the table, and he began to eat. "Don't you want me to taste it first. . . so you'll know it isn't poisoned?"

He shook his head. "It tastes too bad to be poisoned." And again they slept with their backs turned to each other.

A few days later the tailors, father and son, came for the first fitting of Okla's new clothes. He was stripped, shivering before the fireplace, when Portlona ran into the room. He started to speak, then stopped and stared at her. She had fixed her hair in two tight braids and wore bloused, ankle-tied trousers, her "little girl" clothes. "Oh, Cousin Okla, do forgive me for coming in like this but I was just dying to see your new clothes!" She skipped across the room and circled him, humming. "But you don't have any clothes on, do you? I shall just have to wait." She flounced onto the bed and sat, cross-legged, bouncing in time with her humming.

While still wondering what to do, Okla was dressed with silent efficiency by the tailors, then stripped again for additional fitttings. Portlona kept up a running commentary on each garment. "Your little cousin has excellent taste in clothing, sire," the older tailor said.

"My little cousin also has the manners of a peasant," Okla said between his teeth.

The fittings finished, the tailors rolled their materials into bundles and left while Okla hunted for his tousers. "Looking for these, Cousin?" Portlona said, waving them around her head and then flinging them at him from the bed. He caught them and had them up to his knees when she jumped from the bed and grabbed him around the waist, her laughter rising in clear musical tones. "Oh dear cousin, if only you could have seen your face!"

He stood unmoving until, unexpectedly, something warm and good rose in him and he joined her laughter. "But did you see the faces of the tailors. . . especially the old man!" He put his arms around her and rocked back and forth in the pure joy of the moment. She moved her arms up and locked her hands behind his neck, looking up at him. He became still, then tightened his arms and kissed her, long and hard. When it was over they looked at each other, still smiling, then she nestled her face into the hollow of his throat. "Ummm," she said, "I don't think I'm going to be a virgin much longer."

———⬥⬥———

More to relieve the tedium of idleness than out of a desire to be helpful, Okla began to help his father-in-law manage his huge land holdings. This involved long rides to visit resident managers and tenant farmers to collect rents and see to equipment needs. One day, while stopping at a large commune that was almost a self-sufficient village, the older man drew a circle on the table with his finger. "We have now made the complete circle, Okla."

"What do you mean, Uncle Teo?"

"All the land we have visited is owned or controlled by either your father or myself. These connected lands form an unbroken circle around the city and the men who live on these lands are from families of men who served with your father and me in the service of an earlier czar."

"You don't think much of the present czar, do you Uncle Teo?"

"He's a good fighting man, but weak in judgment when the sickness of anger is on him," the old man said, and was silent. Okla felt a thrill as he realized for the first time that his two families, now joined by his marriage, were as powerful as the czar himself. The great circle of land, so painstakingly acquired, could supply the manpower to march on the city itself. And this was why his father was in danger of nothing greater than public disgrace.

Okla met his father several times during the first two years of his marriage, more by accident than by plan. They would hear of him on an adjacent farm and ride an extra half day to find him, usually absorbed in the breeding or training of horses. Their meetings were exuberant and joyful but the conversation would founder after his father asked him if Portlona was pregnant yet. At these times Okla felt guilty and vaguely angry at his wife, knowing the importance of family to his father. He wanted to ask his father when he would make his apologies to the czar so they could reclaim their city house, but he never mustered the courage.

Without being aware of it, Okla gained a respect and affection for the peasants who played as hard as they worked. Nearly all of the men had seen campaign service and kept their skills sharpened by superb horsemanship and rough and tumble wrestling which often erupted into brawling fights. They loved the freedom of the country, lusty living and the raising of large boisterous families. Okla noticed one difference, however, in the lands controlled by his family and those through which they frequently passed. He asked his father-in-law about it. "Why is it that we have no prisoner-workers, Uncle Teo? Almost every place has at least two."

"Your father and I are soldiers, Okla. We don't believe in making slaves of our fellow soldiers."

"But they're prisoners, taken in battle. They belong to us."

"No man belongs to another, Okla. Remember that well." But Okla was not to have time to forget, as his life took a direction he would not have thought possible, even as he pondered and accepted his father-in-law's statement.

The clouds caused near darkness at noon so they left earlier than they had planned. Although they rode through the night, they were caught by the first winter snow and had to pause every quarter hour to rest the horses. Okla, toughened and hardened after two years in the saddle accompanying Uncle Teo, felt only mild discomfort in his numbed feet as he stamped them on the cobbled court yard enroute to his apartment. He entered the back of the building and went directly to the kitchen where he knew it would be warm. Portlona ran to him, helped him out of his coat and knelt to pull his boots off. She sat on the floor, holding his feet in her lap to warm them. "Oh, Okla, I didn't know when you'd get home. The snow is so early this year."

"If we'd waited another day, we'd have had to stay the winter," he said, getting up and walking to the stove. "I'm hungry. What are you cooking?"

"Oh." It was a small sound, muffled by the back of her hand against her mouth.

"Great heavens, girl, you have a lot of food here not to be expecting me. Were you planning to eat it all yourself?"

"That food is for. . . friends."

"Visitors? Why don't they eat at the main house?"

"They're not exactly visitors." She stood up and faced him, afraid yet defiant. "They're prisoners. They ran away. I have them hidden in the other wing, down at the end."

"Have you lost your mind?" he shouted. "Don't you know the penalty for harboring escaped prisoners?"

She stamped her foot. "Nobody will know about it if you'll just stop shouting it to the world! These men are human beings, just like you and me. They don't deserve to be dragged off and killed or, worse yet, be worked to death like animals."

"All right, all right. This will get us nowhere. As long as you have the food fixed, go give it to them. I'll figure out some way to get them out of here after dark."

She sat in a chair, her hands folded in her lap. "Why don't you go on over and kill them now? Then we won't have to waste the food."

He threw his arms over his head. "Now I'm a murderer while my wife risks the ruin of the whole family by hiding runaway prisoners. How long have they been here, anyway?"

"Three days," she said calmly.

"THREE DAYS. . .!"

"Keep your voice down. The poor things were nearly starved when I found them in the old stables. They're stronger now."

Okla composed his face. "That makes me very happy," he said with terribly dignity. "By all means go feed them. I will feed myself and try to sleep for a few blessed hours before the barracks guard breaks in the door."

Okla slept fretfully through the day but when he awoke he knew what his decision would be. When he met the prisoners that evening, the decision had become a commitment in his mind. One of the prisoners was a clear-eyed man in his early thirties who, after five years of captivity, spoke Russian fairly well. The other was a boy about nineteen, younger than Okla, who remained silent although he trembled throughout the brief meeting. Back in their own apartment, Okla asked, "Are there servants here to be trusted?"

"They can all be trusted," Portlona said quietly. "This has happened before."

"How many times?"

"Only once. There were three that time. We gave them food and told them how to leave the country but they were caught and killed."

"Does Uncle Teo know about this?"

"My father? I don't think so. What are you thinking, Okla?"

He looked back into her eyes, his face relaxed and thoughtful and she knew his mind had not yet perceived her question. She searched her own mind as she watched him, trying to isolate and understand the completeness she felt when with him. The word, 'spiritual' was in her vocabulary but she discarded it when it came to her mind at these times, thinking of the loutish priests and monks who had come to her home during her schooling and taught a strange dichotomy of love for a benevolent Christ overshadowed by a vengeful and vile-tempered God. Even in the soft warmth following their love-making she would often yearn for what she thought of as the light which was never struck, a light always there but never quite seen. She saw his eyes change, become clearer and sharp. "I want you to send a messenger to my father. I know where he is."

"You think your father would help?"

Okla laughed. "I know he will. This will put some real adventure into the old boy's life. We can send our messenger in the small sleigh now and they could be back by late tomorrow night."

Within an hour a stable boy rode out with the sleigh, the horse's hooves muffled and the runners hissing over the now partially packed snow. The following night, before dawn, Okla's father stumped into their bedroom and roughed them out of bed. "Have you taken leave of your senses?" he greeted them with a mild roar.

"But father, I felt sure you would want to help these men. . ."

"Oh, damn those men," the old man said. "And damn you, too. I mean, what's the idea of sending a man for me without sending even a dram of vodka to warm my innards? Ha?"

Portlona scrambled out of bed. "There's vodka in the kitchen. I'll get it for you."

"I'll fetch it myself. Get yourselves dressed. We've work to do."

Later the old soldier squatted on his haunches and handed a cup of vodka to the prisoners, which they drank gratefully. "Which of you speaks our language?" he said.

The older man stood up. "I speak some, sire."

"Good. You will drive a sleigh load of feed grain to a farm a day's ride from here." He turned and faced his son. "It's where you were married." He looked again at the prisoner. "You will drive while your friend and I doze under the grain bags and drink your share of the vodka. Portlona! Do you have a big sleigh ready?"

"It hasn't been brought out this year but I'm sure it is ready. Our equipment is always in good condition."

The old man slapped her on the rump and she winced. "So's mine!" he said. "Well, get moving, girl. I want to be underway by first light."

The older prisoner stepped near. "Excuse me, sire. I do not completely understand. We have just run away from a farm, yet you are sending us to another. We had just as soon give ourselves up and die rather than face a short lifetime of labor in your country."

Okla's father towered over the man, his fists on his hips. "The farm you are going to belongs to me, and my son's family. We do not believe in killing soldier-prisoners, even a former enemy, so we cannot accommodate you in that department. You may live and work at the farm if you like. If you do not find it congenial, no hand will be raised to stay you if you want to leave. You might even find your way back to your own home."

Tears came to the prisoner's eyes and he knelt. "I am sorry, sire. I did not understand." He looked up. "But will you not be endangering your own people?"

"Ha! My people have no great love for the czar and the czar dares not send his troops onto my land. Now hurry, man. Change into these clothes and help load the sleigh."

— ❦ —

Near the end of the year Okla came home late after an afternoon of drinking mulled wine with school-days friends he now felt free to associate with. The large kettle was bubbling in the steamy kitchen. He shrugged out of his coat but left his boots on. He sighed. "More prisoners?" She nodded. "How many this time?" he said.

"Four," she said brightly. "Or there should be four by now. Two came at first dark and when they found out we would help them, told me of two more hiding in the forest. One has gone to get them."

He cut a piece of bread and ate it against the sourness of the wine in his stomach. "How did they find out?"

"I don't know. None of them speaks Russian." She came to him and put her hands behind his neck in the now familiar and well loved gesture. "But the important thing is that we must help them." It was a simple statement, not a question.

In this moment he knew his way, and with a sweet, certain sadness knew where the way would ultimately take them. He held her close. "Yes, dear heart, we must help them." He held her from him. "How are they? Will they be able to travel by morning?"

"They have come far and are tired, but not weak like the others. But can your father be here by morning?"

"I will take them myself and send word for my father to meet me on the road. I must learn the way for those who will come in the future. I will go now and make the sleigh ready."

She worked with him through the night, laying boards to form a false floor for the sleigh so the prisoners could huddle beneath it in reasonable warmth if not in comfort. With an axe, they hurriedly hacked chunks of meat from frozen carcasses of deer and calves hanging in the storehouse. These would be thawed and cooked on an iron charcoal brazier which would be kept burning on the floor of the sleigh. The sleigh vanished instantly in the jet darkness of pre-dawn but she stood until chilled, facing the direction it had gone. Reviving the kitchen fire without arousing the servants, she sought to warm herself, but the chill remained as she thought of Okla and the daylight part of the journey he must make in the conspicuous four-horse sleigh through territory peopled by those of questionable loyalty. Later, she knew, they would find safer routes but now, until her man returned, hopefully within the week, it would not be easy to warm herself.

<hr>

When they had been married five years, Uncle Teo died of pneumonia after an illness of only two days. Sitting propped in bed to relieve the painful congestion in his chest, he stoically received the last rites of the Orthodox Church. Okla and Portlona entered as the priest finished. "He refused to make his confession," the priest whispered shaking his head.

Uncle Teo overheard. "I haven't that much time. Okla, get that spoiler of souls out of here so I can make my farewells before coughing my bloody lungs out."

Portlona took his hand. "It was your idea to send for the priest, father. You know that neither Okla nor I nor my brother hold much with the Church."

"I couldn't have a state funeral without him," the dying man said.

"Is that so important to you?"

The man coughed and retched into a cloth, his forehead shiny with sweat. "More important to you than to me," he said when he could speak. "Can't afford to further antagonize our glorious leader. Bring me some vodka in hot water with some of that spice stuff in it."

Portlona slipped out to prepare the drink and Uncle Teo motioned for Okla to sit. "Okla, my son will retire as commander of the guards and assume the management of this estate."

Okla did not feel he knew his brother-in-law, Uncle Teo's only living son. An impressive, physically powerful man twice Okla's age, 'the brother' as he was called by all, spoke little but had embraced Okla warmly when Okla was formally presented to the family after the wedding. The first family dinner had lasted until daylight, but Okla remembered that the brother had left early to personally supervise the midnight changing of the palace guard, and that he had drunk little during an evening of revelry. It was not ambition but almost faultless competence which had earned the brother the rank of General at an early age while Okla's father, quite happily, had served as the czar's Colonel of Security. The brother was second only to the czar himself in power, and Okla wondered why Uncle Teo would ask him to relinquish this post of popular prominence.

In honesty, Okla admitted that he was young in years and experience but he also knew his learning had been conscientious and thorough, "Are you displeased with my work, Uncle Teo?" he said.

Okla, startled, was sure he had seen a glint of amusement in the pain-filled eyes. He was right. The old man chuckled and said, "No, Okla, I am very pleased with your work." He put his hand out to indicate he wanted to rest, then closed his eyes. "Wait till your wife returns," he whispered.

Portlona entered the room a few minutes later with the steaming drink in a heavy pewter mug, wrapped with cloth to preserve the heat. Uncle Teo opened his eyes. "Ah, that'll put a few more hours of life into me." He sipped the drink as Portlona sat on the arm of Okla's chair, her arm around his shoulders, "How many prisoners have you aided in the past three years?" the old man said in a stronger voice than before. Okla jumped and nearly spilled Portlona onto the floor.

She resettled herself, musing. "About a hundred, I'd say. . . wouldn't you Okla?"

Okla swallowed. "A hundred and three, not counting the three who died on us last winter. But Uncle Teo, how did you know?" He glared at Portlona. "Did you tell him?"

"We have never mentioned it till this moment," Uncle Teo said. "Okla, Okla, I have been growing old but not foolish. Too much of your energy is going to the poor wretches we have taken from their homes and too little to the management of the most powerful house in the land. For all of our sakes, we must protect this house. Hush. I have more to say and I am becoming very tired. You must no longer use this house. It is too dangerous now that the city is growing in this direction. I think the brother also knows but you must consider his position, his family and the families of my other daughters. I have land in the great forest west of the city. I acquired it for the timber but the operation was not profitable so I abandoned it. There is a road leading there and a house of sorts."

Portlona nodded, remembering being taken there by the brother when she was a child. The site was only about two hours from the city and not far off the main road. The area was so densely wooded, however, that the few attempts to clear it, as her father's attempt, had been abandoned. It would be an ideal place from which to expand their operation and, as her father said, much safer. "Rest now, father," she said. "I know what we shall do. . . rebuild the house as a summer house. They are becoming quite popular now."

"But how do we get word to the prisoners?" Okla said.

"How do we ever get word to them? Have you been out recruiting them?" She took her father's hand. "We will leave you now, father. Is there anything else?"

He inclined his head to Okla and put his other hand on Okla's arm. "My best to your father. He would have enjoyed my funeral."

Okla's father DID enjoy the funeral. He was present, huge and grizzled, standing in the cathedral with Uncle Teo's family. . . and in uniform! After the ceremony, the czar and czarina began to lead the procession up the aisle. Dark-visaged, the czar paused beside Okla's father. "You have great temerity presenting yourself to this assemblage, Colonel."

Okla's father bowed low. "I come only to pay final respects to a dear friend. I have heard no public proclamation forbidding me to wear this uniform although, most Excellent Pontificate, you will notice I am not wearing my orders."

The czar grunted and moved on. The czarina delayed to place a soft hand on Okla's arm. "Will you wait on me a week from today?" she said. Unable to speak, Okla nodded. "In the afternoon," she said, and followed her husband out of the church.

Okla's father, with thirty or forty old soldier cronies, returned with the family to Uncle Teo's home. They drank throughout the night and made the old house vibrate with their noise. "Wherever he is, I hope Uncle Teo isn't trying to sleep," Okla muttered from his bed as another Cossack marching song began.

After he was sober, Okla's father had no inkling concerning the czarina's invitation. He furthermore professed to have little interest in it and lent his gusto to plans for the new hideaway. He knew the area and pronounced the present house worthless unless, he mused, a secret underground room could be built under it. Okla left him, knowing that despite the aura of confusion which seemed to surround his father's activities, the house would be built, and probably in record time.

Half fearfully, Okla presented himself at the palace at the appointed time and was immediately shown to the czarina's private chambers. He bowed, as he had seen his father do, and said, "Your servant, Most Excellent Pontificate."

She nodded, smiled and asked him to sit. "I hope I am not intruding on the mourning period for your father-in-law," she said. Okla looked at her warily and she laughed. "We have known of your marriage for some time, Okla. It is a pity you have no children yet. That would have pleased Teo. . . and would have given your father excuse for a truly memorable brawl."

"About my father. . ." Okla felt his face burning.

She reached her hand to his arm. "Your father is a very valued friend and always shall be. But I did not ask you here to talk of your father."

"Yes, Excellency?"

"I understand you are one of our budding intellectuals."

"I do not know what intellectual means, Excellency. I meet with school comrades once or twice a month at the Wolf's Head Inn for wine and talk."

"It is the talk which interests me, Okla. No, no," she put out a hand as he started to protest. "I am not concerned with what you talk about, only that there are still those in Russia who keep their minds alive."

Okla smiled. "Some of our discussions are in reality quite lively."

"That is good. I have thoughts of starting a university in the city dedicated to the study of the Arts and Literature. Oh, I know we have an excellent tutorial system but that is limited to the wealthy. I would like to see a place where all who are interested will have a place to study."

Okla thought of the brawling tradesmen's sons, the builders whose backs and shoulders were bunched with muscle, the dull-eyed laborers from the tile works--THESE, as students?!

He considered the idea quite mad but told the czarina he thought it splendid.

"Fine!" She clapped her hands. "Then do this for me: discuss my plans with your friends and see if there are those among you who would like to become teachers. Yourself, for instance."

"I participate but am never a leader of our discussions, Excellency, although there are those who I am sure would welcome the opportunity."

"Good. Bring them to me when you find it convenient."

Okla's friends were enthusiastic and, with him, made a number of visits to the czarina in the years that followed. It was not until after the czarina's death, however, that her dreams materialized.

The years blended into each other for Okla and Portlona. Their underground escape channel became so well organized that they knew it could continue without them, although they did not discuss this when making this safeguard. Personal danger was so much a way of life that they reacted instinctively rather than rationally to threats. They selected their cadres with care, almost wholly from former soldiers who had served under Okla's father, men and their families who loved the old Colonel more fiercely than they understood the tenets of freedom which motivated the freeing of the prisoners. Some were careless and were caught and fought the czar's guards until they died. Others were stripped of their possessions and exiled from the czar's domain, to survive or perish in a harsh and alien environment. But only twice, reluctantly, were Okla and Portlona forced to order the death of those who would turn informer.

Opening new avenues as old ones became known, Okla rode to the frontier a dozen times, memorizing his routes and translating them into maps when he returned home. He returned from one such month-long trip and Portlona greeted him as always, by removing his boots and holding his feet in her lap. "The snow will be early again this year," he said. "Wouldn't surprise me if it starts tonight. Say, girl, why so quiet? I told you I'd be home in time for my thirtieth birthday."

"There is news from the city," she said. "Your so-called radical intellectual friends tried to kill the czar."

"No! Did they actually make the attempt?"

"I don't think so. They were planning to take over the palace and someone told the czar."

"Sounds serious."

"Serious enough to land them all in prison," she said. "I'm afraid there's more. Do you want to hear it now?"

"Tell me while you fix the food," he said, splashing some vodka into a cup and drinking it off.

"A proclamation was read over the city today. It seems too many prisoner-workers have been escaping, especially from the tile-works. Guard troops will ride out every day and night and circle the city. You know what that means, Okla."

He rubbed his eyes. "I could think better if I weren't so damnably tired. Yes, I know. We must leave this house. We had best ride out in the morning. We will be safe within the great circle." He looked around. "It will be a shame to leave this house after nearly eight years."

She came to stand beside him. "Yes, but you have often said yourself that we have been safe here because of the laziness of the guards rather than our own cleverness."

Okla walked to the outhouse. A dozen years of stress and danger rushed into Portlona's mind, even as she tried to push it away. Weakened for the moment, she sat on a crude stool near the fireplace, her fingers unconsciously trying to smooth the deep wrinkles which had formed around her eyes, age-marks not befitting a wealthy young matron of only twenty-eight. And again she sought words to implant an intelligent line of reasoning to support the course of action she had taken, and into which she had led her mate. Her love of luxury and ease still caused her to despise the soundly built but crude log house in the deserted forest where most of her life was spent, alone and waiting. Whence then, came the compulsion to continue with it? Hundreds of prisoner-laborers had been returned to freedom, many to their own lands, others to wilderness areas to the South where the more adventurous were there building new colonies and showing promise of succeeding as a new force taking their livelihood from the abundance to be found in the tree-choked, unmapped forests.

But the futility of it all closed around her like the rare times of summer heat and stifling humidity. They kept no records but she knew they had effected the release/escape of hundreds, probably between one and two thousand. Yet there were tens of thousands of the prisoner-laborers still in the land, the numbers increased by occasional border raids by ruthless men who sold their captives into bondage. Why, then, did they continue, never at rest, never at peace, already beginning to grow old?

You wanted it this way, a voice said in her mind. Yes, she answered, but I did not think it would be this difficult. She jerked herself erect, self-conscious because she had spoken aloud. It will soon end, the voice in her mind persisted, and then you will understand. You will understand it all. She stood and began to prepare their meal. At least that will be a relief, she said, again speaking aloud and with a return of her high good humor. Okla returned to the house. "I wish we had a sleigh here. It's beginning to snow. . . what's that!" He ran from the house, she stood in the doorway. "We have visitors, Portlona," he called from the darkness. "Prepare more food."

While the three prisoners ate and warmed themselves, Okla went outside again. "The snow has stopped. Unless they came through the forest, their tracks will lead directly here. Can you find out?" Okla had never learned the language of the Balkans while Portlona, with gestures, could communicate.

"They're too frightened to understand," she said. "What can we do? We have only the two horses and no sleigh. We can't just leave them here."

"Tear the blankets and wrap their feet. They will have to walk." He put out his hand. "Never mind," he said quietly. "It's too late." Then she, too, heard the sound of many horses approaching the house.

The guards battered the door open before the leather fastener could be loosed. The leader stepped through, followed by a half dozen more and they stood, blinking in the sudden light. "Oh ho, so it's the rich who have betrayed their country," the leader shouted. "I wish we had the authority to kill them on the spot. Bind them quickly. There'll be triple rations of vodka for everybody this night!" Okla, who still wore his knee-length coat, reached Portlona's cape to her. A guard knocked it from his hand to the floor. Portlona gave the man such a withering look of contempt that he retreated a few steps. With complete dignity, she got her cape from the floor and with deliberate motions, put it on. Neither spoke as the guards wrapped lengths of coarse rope around them and yanked it tight.

"What about our guests?" Okla said, indicating the prisoners.

"These scum?" the leader said. "Oh, we'll give THEM a warm time. Burn the house!"

"But you can't just burn them alive," Portlona said, as the wall by the fireplace began to blaze.

The leader looked at her and laughed. "You're perfectly right, rich lady. We won't burn them. You men, take these swine outside and strip them! They won't need clothes with a nice warm fire to warm themselves by. Here. . .. burn their clothes!" They mounted and waited until the entire house was blazing, then turned to the road. One of the naked prisoners hesitantly followed the group a few paces, until a guard reared his horse and ran him down.

Hours later, in the city, they were taken to an unheated barracks building with windows boarded up on the outside and thrown inside. They collided with other bodies and fell, kicked and cursed by those they landed on. A candle was lit and a bearded young man Okla's age came and squatted beside him. "Okla," he said. "Dear friend of the czarina. What did YOU do, try to kill the old bastard on your own? We haven't seen you since last year."

"Untie us first and then we can talk," Okla said. He told them, briefly, why he and Portlona had been brought there. When he told of helping the prisoner-workers to escape, there was much excitement. "You should have told us, Okla," one said. "We would have helped you."

"Perhaps I should have," Okla said. "At least it would have taken your minds off killing the czar."

"Oh, we weren't going to kill him. Just depose him."

Okla rubbed the circulation back into his arms. "I doubt that. But who were you going to put in his place?"

"Your brother-in-law," several said at once.

"The brother! Didn't you dunces know he was retired several years ago?"

"He would have done it, Okla. Never fear. Your father was the one who suggested him."

"My father! What does he have to do with all this?"

"Well, he talked to us some. . ."

"Where is he now?"

"Somewhere in the palace. He was arrested soon after we were."

Okla groaned, his head in his hands. "That finishes it."

"But why? You and your father are reputed to be almost as wealthy as the czar himself. Surely you can find some way to save us."

"Never mind. Let's try to sleep." Okla held Portlona until she slept, then assessed their situation. Banishment, for sure, but they could probably live in seclusion in some rural area of the protectorate without molestation. He could not help the others, even if he had desired to do so in the face of their stupidity. Ah well, it would all be resolved at their trial. The judges, although appointed by the czar, had a reputation for fairness and scrupulous adherence to the meager laws existing under a military regime.

In the morning they were beaten awake by the guards and hustled to a larger hall. The word spread among them like a flash of lightening. . .they were to have an audience with the czarina! They were made to remain standing and warned to make no sound. Accompanied by the captain of the guards, the czarina made her way to a small stage at the end of the room. Okla marked that her grace and kindness was still manifest although she was growing heavy as the years advanced. She began to speak. "I am disappointed in you. I had hoped to instill constructive attitudes in you rather than a spirit of destruction. However, you have helped me lay the groundwork for the university which is still uppermost in my mind. With this in mind, I have spoken to my husband and he has assured me he will not insist on prison sentences. In this you are fortunate. In having to leave your homes, you are unfortunate. I am sorry for you." At her signal, the guard captain motioned Okla and Portlona forward. The others were taken away.

Okla bowed but remained silent. "I am sorry to see you and your lovely wife enmeshed in this," the czarina said. "But banishment should not sit heavily on you, Okla. You have scarcely been seen in the city for years." She paused, then frowned when the guard captain whispered to her. "My husband wishes to talk with you immediately so you must go. I will talk to you before your trial. I expect you will be released on your honor and not confined."

"She apparently doesn't know about our prisoner dealings," Portlona said after the czarina left the room. "Do you think she will still be able to help us when she finds out?"

"I expect so," Okla said. "The czar is an unpredictable man but she has a powerful influence on him."

Okla was not surprised to see his father when they entered the czar's rooms. The old man stood with arms folded across his chest. The knuckles of both hands were bruised and lacerated and there were several deep gashes on his face, now scabbed over, and a deep purpling extended from his chin to his temple. Okla wondered how many guards were still in the infirmary after THIS arrest. He then looked at the czar and almost recoiled. The big man's face was mottled with dark red splotches, a trickle of saliva ran from a corner of his mouth into his close-cropped beard. His eyes were quite insane.

"You, Colonel, have defied me for the last time!" the czar hissed.

"I am prepared to stand trial for my activities," the old man said.

"There will be no trial! You will rot in prison!"

"There is still the law, Excellency," Okla's father said. "Your law."

"There is no law sufficient to punish a wretch who spawns traitors to their own country." The czar's voice was high-pitched and choked. He shifted his mad eyes to Okla. "There are no words for the likes of you so I will save my breath. Send for the priest!" The last words were almost screamed and even Okla's father twitched at the sound.

The old man moved involuntarily and was instantly surrounded by four worried guards with drawn swords. "What are you going to do, Excellency?"

"I'm going to execute them, you fool! And don't talk to me of the law. I am the law!" His voice dropped almost to a whisper. "But I am the law tempered with compassion. The aiding of escaping prisoners is an offense punishable by death in any land. I have been too lenient in not enforcing it before. Hell is too good for them, but you will take note that I have ordered a priest to try to intercede for their miserable souls."

As if awaiting these words, the priest came in, trembling violently and half-carried by a guard at each elbow. He selected a chair, spread the altar cloth on it and accepted help from a guard in lighting the candles. He motioned to Portlona, but she had to be forced to her knees, her eyes wide and unbelieving. Okla stepped forward and knelt beside her. "As we have lived together and will die together, so we will take the last sacrament together."

Okla took a deep ragged breath and clenched his hands because he knew they had begun to tremble. He had faced death several times fighting the half savage guards the czar assigned to patrol the border, but there had been the exultation of reckless physical combat. Now there was only sadness, knowing his life was ending pointlessly and at the whim of a deranged mind. The priest could slip quietly to the czarina's apartment and, with a few words, the nightmare could be halted. But, looking at the fear-crazed priest, Okla felt more pity than contempt, knowing the craven man feared for his life more than anything else. It began to come to him, vaguely at first then with a growing calmness, that they had not failed. In some way he was soon to understand, the course they had taken was not through choice; there had been no alternative, and as they had been joined in life, they could not be separated by death. All fear now drained from him, he looked up at the priest, waiting.

"This is highly irregular," the priest said.

"Do it man," Okla's father roared. "Or the beast will have your head taken off, too."

"Beast, am I?" the czar shrieked. "I suppose you want the same."

The old man bowed a final time in magnificent mockery. "When you cut down a man's only son, you take the man's life."

The czar pounded the arm of his chair with the flat of his hand. "I am the taker of life this day! So be it. Kneel there with your criminal children!"

The old soldier folded his arms again and smiled. "I need no mumbo-jumbo from this blubbering idiot. I am at peace."

These final words plucked through the numbness of Portlona's brain. Peace. Yes. It was over now. No more starting from bed at a sudden sound in the night. No anxiety awaiting Okla when he was away from her. And in a sudden thrilling second of clarity, she saw that her love for Okla and his for her would live on, out of the bounds of time, ever growing and expanding. . . deathless. With almost detached interest, she recalled the stirrings she had occasionally felt with him, an almost-remembering of ponderous eras of time without measure. She glanced sideways at his face, recalling other times she had seen it, waking but somehow as in a dream when the features were recognizable yet subtly different, tinged with ancient familiarity and always, always with her. The nearness of the ultimate realization brought an excitement that softened the lines in her face and made it glow as it had when she had been surprised with a gift as a child. She had lived, during the years with Okla, in such continuous physical fear and dull dread that nothing of it remained, and for this she was thankful. She searched her mind for words to tell Okla of this wonder which filled her, but the quietness in his face told her that words were no longer necessary. Almost shyly, she took her mate's hand and smiled at him. "Hurry, old man," she said to the priest, and suppressed a giggle when the priest's head popped up like a cork from a bottle of new wine.

The executions were carried out an hour later in a secret cellar of the palace and the bodies were carried away and quickly buried, unmarked, in the great forest west of the city. Yet by afternoon, the knowledge was spread throughout the city and the people grew quiet and fearful. This was the first execution of anyone of such high rank in anyone's memory, and the first without a trial in a hundred years.

The czar conducted no business that day but sat alone, nursing his fury, because to release it would have opened him to the terror of what he had done. He had acquired his position of power because he possessed a superior intelligence which enabled him to channel this berserk rage with an intense singleness of purpose. He infected his followers with this magnetic ferocity and no opposition had been able to stand against him. He embraced Christianity with an amused cynicism because he believed the Church's power rested in utilizing superstition while he, in turn, could use the Church to HIS personal advantage. He monopolized the teachers who journeyed to instruct the clergy in what he regarded as HIS Church and was therefore more highly educated than the priests or the leaders of the poverty-ridden monastic orders he supported to furnish teachers to the families of the landed classes, the nucleus of a future aristocracy.

He had never conquered his wife, the daughter of a proud baron in the land of the Goths whom he had killed in honorable single combat. He took her as a child of thirteen but did not take her to his bed until their marriage was sanctified by a priest nearly seven years later. He could not comprehend love but somehow knew that his furious torments would destroy him if he did not have her cheerful and soothing voice to bring him to reason when the blackness came upon him. There were no battles to be fought for a decade and the boredom of administering a domain of peace would have caused him to ruin it with manufactured violence had she not shown him the pleasures to be had from manufactured dignity and the pageantry of court life in which she carefully tutored him.

Toward nightfall, when his physical strength could no longer sustain his anger, he forced himself to rise and walk the long silent corridors to their sleeping apartment, a red nausea rising to blind his eyes when he knew he would have to face her with what he had done. He paused outside the curtained bedroom but pushed his way inside when he heard a tired, dry sobbing.

The czarina lay on her back, her face ugly and contorted with the poison which had killed her a few hours before. Her personal maid sat on the floor, her face swollen with weeping. "She's dead," the girl said, her voice hoarse.

The czar made no move. "What happened?"

The girl scooted on the floor, away from him. "She said. . . she said when you killed those people you killed her. She wrote a letter." The words came in a rush as she thrust a roll of paper into his hand.

"Why didn't you send for me?"

"I meant to die with her, Sire, but. . . I couldn't."

"That's all right, child," he said with infinite weariness and held his hand to help her to her feet. She looked at the hand, screamed and ran from the room.

———————— ▭ ◁————————

The young liberals were banished for life, as prescribed by the law, although they were permitted to retain adequate monies and possessions to assure that their exile would not be hurtful. Because of the unrest of the country people loyal to Okla's family, his brother-in-law was prudently coaxed out of retirement and placed in command of the army. This meant he was the Regent, virtual ruler of the country; the broken czar subsided into melancholia and only appeared on state occasions. Under the new Regent the czarina's university was begun, all prisoner-workers were released and many chose to remain in the more productive land with their freedom. The army planned no new campaigns.

The Regent was a pragmatic man whose stern self-discipline allowed no latitude for the superstitious nonsense of religion or the inner disruptions of consciousness he sometimes heard referred to as 'the spirit'. Nevertheless, as age and more frequent fatigue closed around him, he would often stay alone in his chambers late at night, savoring a flagon of good wine. Permitting himself the luxury of jesting at himself during these times, he would review the progress of the land--no confiscation of private possessions for waging war, no men held in slavery forced to perform tasks they would do willingly if they could enjoy the results of their labor, an occasional meeting with other czars to formulate agreements to guarantee safe passage through each other's domains. The Regent was an austere man and opened his thoughts to no person but, mellowed with wine, he would say softly, "Well, Okla, do you see? Have we done well?" And sometimes, when the wine had given a peculiar clearness to his brain, he thought he heard an answer, "Yes, brother, we have done well--

"For this time--"

———————— ▭ ◁————————

Examining the lives of Okla and Portlona, we became very fond of them, a couple of rich kids thrust into a life situation neither of them ever understood. We are still too hazy concerning the true significance of what happened to us as Okla and Portlona to draw any firm conclusions. The meeting and mating was apparently one of our easiest; it simply involved the selection of receptive vehicles (parents) within the framework of a beginning aristocracy in a sparsely populated country. In retrospect, we feel we accomplished a great deal in the way of spiritual advancement, or at least cancelled a lot of karma accumulated in past lifetimes. We know there must have been urgent, even stringent reasons for such frequent returns to earthly life. While we don't yet know the complete background, we have had enough intimations to suspect there must have been quite a burden on our etheric consciences. It is a relief, therefore, to know that we were successful in our avowed purpose to make some sort of amends when we entered life in the persons of Okla and Portlona.

The circumstances of their deaths were so shocking and surprising that we were filled with a sense of outrage -- we didn't want it to be this way, although we believe those young people had premonitions of a violent end, even at the beginning of their dangerous undertaking. Our life styles in our current lifetime are on the conservative side and we don't anticipate perilous challenges to our physical courage. But it's comforting to know we've got the old zip and zing in us (somewhere) in case we ever should need it.

"This is the Keetoowah." That's the gravel-voiced greeting I have come to anticipate when I pick up the phone. Looking at these other lives from a different perspective, we encountered a delightful new game. . . WHERE is the Keetoowah? How does he fit into this particular lifetime? There seems to be a sort of family hierarchy in the spirit realm, compatible souls who may have chosen to be together forever. And this includes reincarnating with a deliberate plan to share this family relationship during an earth life. We know that Keetoowah is family so when we now look into another incarnation, we always look for him. Quietly protective, Keetoo-wah as Uncle Teo entered the world and benevolently shadowed the lives of Okla and Portlona until they no longer needed him.

We have reviewed, and continue to look into other lifetimes whenever a new encounter or situation provides the stimulus. Keetoowah does not appear in all of them, or even a majority of them. Since he claims to have been aware of the 20th Century Harry Green for a number of years prior to our physical reunion, I strongly feel he was actively present on another level of consciousness while these past life histories were being selected. If a part of his fragmented spirit was hanging around in 1972 when the compilation of data was going on, he is indeed a prime contributor to this work.

I have not yet come upon a satisfactory explanation (to me) of why this re-grouping of souls on the earth plane happens. It could be that these spirits stay together because they like each other. That doesn't hold, however, when you realize that enemies also return on the same earthtime plane. Or, it could be they came back to work out the karma of this enmity. Or, maybe to get in another lick at the old so-and-so? The transition from earth life to spirit doesn't automatically entail a reformation of character.

I had a personal experience with this phenomenon a few years ago. Traveling through New Mexico, we stopped for an overnight visit with an old college chum whom I hadn't seen for nearly seventeen years. We had enjoyed an unusually warm friendship in school, had seen each other a time or two since then, had kept track of each other although our correspondence was desultory. Frank and I (I will call him Frank because that's his name) had followed similar careers, were both reasonably successful and the reunion was as joyful as we had both hoped for.

I have always been aware of out-of-body experiences, the first one I can recall when I was six years old. Although I still can't control them, that doesn't prevent me from enjoying them and I was pressed to share with Frank my memories of other-level trips I had made with him off and on during the years since we had seen each other. He gaped at me and before I was well begun he interrupted, "Sure, I remember that, but I thought it was just a vivid dream!" We took it from there, filling in remembered details, corroborating each other, exulting in proving to each other that it really happened. Frank had had only a dormant interest in such matters; he accepted the psychic but was more interested in raising pure-bred cats. With due solemnity, we agreed that it was unlikely that two people could have identical dreams when separated by years and ten thousand miles. . . much of this happened when I lived in Europe and he lived in Oregon.

A nagging thought persisted and I put it to him some time later. Why was there no strangeness, no 'warming up' to each other? Even at our age, seventeen years is a pretty good chunk out of anyone's life, yet we were as easy and familiar and close to each other as if we had seen each other the day before yesterday. The most cogent reply to this question came from his wife, a lovely person who stated, quite simply, "You were no stranger in this house." Having prompted Frank in a few basic tricks of recall, he contributed notes from a casual diary he'd kept since our last meeting, impressions of awareness of me and Carol and of our surroundings. On the points we could verify without doubt, he was 80% correct. No wonder I wasn't a stranger if I had been nosing around their lives that much.

At their request, I set my spirit research team to work to try to determine the wherefores of our immediate and apparently continuing closeness to each other. The item of least interest to emerge was that Frank is something like a great, great grandfather of mine, in direct lineal descent. When one considers the mathematical probability of how many males have diffused my personal blood line within the past two or three hundred years, the grandfather thing isn't very impressive. Of more interest was the fact that Frank and I have shared a bond which, in the words of my informant, 'exists beyond the limits of measurable time'. We have shared many earth lifetimes, most frequently with he as my father, a dubious honor he shares with Keetoowah. For example, I was told he was my father in the Russian lifetime of Okla and Portlona. I am not easily flabbergasted but I indulged myself on this one. Old Frank, devoted husband and provider, raiser of cats who votes Republican. . . dearly beloved friend though he is, could he have been the half-wild Cossack cavalry-man? Yet, when I took the time to project my memory back to that time, I recognized him.

As for his wife's gentle bewilderment as to my familiarity in their home, this was easily accounted for. She recognized me from the many times when I came to pick Frank up for one of our other-worldly jaunts; it took only a slight prodding to trigger this memory, to bring it to the surface from her subconscious. Wives being what they are, ours no doubt wonder just what we're up to at these times. So do we, but all I have been able to garner is that we visit some of those areas 'beyond the limits of measurable time', a pilgrimage back to the old homestead, as it were, in some realm of the vastness of the universe which will probably never be charted by our race. And yes, of course, all four of us have known each other for many earth lifetimes.

V

When Carol and I came together one of our first mutual interests was found to be a recurring and frequent consuming absorption with ancient Egypt. This was further whetted by reading the masterful Joan Grant's 'far memory' books on Egypt, THE WINGED PHAROAH and others. Miss Grant is a superb stylist and can be read and appreciated for that alone, but Carol and I both responded with an uncanny familiarity to and identity with Miss Grant's accounts of an earlier, lush and fertile Egypt.

It could be expected, therefore, that when we began our exploration of past shared lives, we would land on the Poet with both feet and demand, "Egypt!"

I cannot describe the way in which the Poet and I communicate. He flashes ideas and visual images which I translate into words. Yes, the Poet said, you lived a number of lifetimes in ancient Egypt. And if you exercised a bit more self-discipline now in meditation and prayer, a lot more would be available to your present-day memories. We were thus chided by a number of our friends in spirit when we got down to earnest work. Carol usually responded by dissolving into a storm of furious tears; I would vent my own repressed childishness by storming at Carol. It wasn't easy, any of it, but it has made us better people.

This Egyptian thing took a lot of sorting out. We learned that many lifetimes, over a dozen, had been entered with the express purpose of placing ourselves into positions of ease and affluence. We jumped at this enthusiastically; it would make a great reading. The Poet squelched this by reminding us that not only had Joan Grant done it better than we could, she was a far more admirable person during parallel times. We, apparently, were rich, privileged and threw our weight around with obnoxious sloppiness.

This propensity to repeatedly insert ourselves into the upper crust seems to be a weakness nursed along from time immemorial. It appears that we were rarely able to carry it off successfully, which might account for a certain amount of chagrin and a stubborn determination to stick with it through successive incarnations in the face of our obvious incompetence in these areas of earthly existence. In brief, the Poet asked us if we really wanted to relate the histories of a couple of snot-noses who dipped in and out of Egyptian aristocracy for a thousand years or more. When it was put this way, we began to wonder if we had ever done anything worthwhile. The answer of course is yes, but only if we learned something worthwhile from that particular life experience. This answer is also known only to us, as a personal and private part of our own eternal memories. We do not have the facilities to tap these memories but the Poet thinks the lives of Hedoterus and Kismé which follow are the result of a time when we became so thoroughly ashamed of our repeated self indulgences that we thrust ourselves into situations of relative humility.

We are still going over these lives, quite soberly because we have been told they were the last ones lived in Egypt. No doubt they were. The agricultural descriptions received from our spirit historians indicate that Egypt at the time of our story had declined to where the only area of floral fertility lay along the Nile valley, extending to its source in what is still the beginning of tropical Africa. Turnabouts in ecological history do not happen as casually as we observe them when traversing the world at ten miles a minute in a jet, but they do occur at recordable evolutionary periods. We believe we, in Egypt, lived through a fragment of one of these periods as Kismé (Kiss-may) and Hedoterus.

Neighbors stopped to share a cup and rejoice with the families of the Oriane brothers when the first child was born to the younger brother. The river was at flood, a great flood after three dry years. The Oriane brothers, more industrious and prosperous than most, slogged happily through the mud and channeled the spreading water to fields which had been abandoned to them by despairing neighbors during the dry years. They bartered for more seed grain and sat long into the night working on details of the planting. Then to the youngor, his first born, and a son! The river gods were smiling; a special prayer of thanksgiving was lifted to the fertility gods for the new man child. He was named Hedoterus to honor the grandfather who had died of the fever only last year.

Thirty miles down the river and within the same fortnight a girl baby was born to the weary parents of ten, who had fervently hoped each of the last three would be the last. Because the parents were well-to-do owners of horses which towed empty boats up the great river after they had negotiated the sale of their harvests in the city, unctuous relatives came to pay their formal respects, hoping for the honor of having their family name given to the child. The child's mother, tired and worn at thirty-five, indulged herself in a rare whimsey and named the child for ALL the relatives, then announced to the family that the child would be known as Kismé, or good-luck-piece. The mother kept to herself the reservation that 'good-luck-piece' would hopefully be the final offering of the fertility gods. The child's father took scant interest in the affair, not even objecting when his wife took the prerogative of naming the child. After all, of what use was yet another girl? Just one more mouth to feed.

The family of Hedoterus lived in a house which was more an agglomeration of rooms than a planned home. Older sections of the structure crumbled and fell with age; the stones were reused for more modern rooms with larger windows and higher ceilings. Although ownership of the property was re-established every ten years by affirmation of the reigning pharoah, none knew the history of the land since none could read and written records were meaningless. They were aware that some ancestor whose memory had passed into oblivion had built the hillock of stone and earth on which the house stood to be above the waters of the annual flood. Once probably flat, the hillock had eroded and changed shape with the centuries. New construction followed the contours of the land so the present house stood with no two rooms on the same level, a delight to generations of children but a subliminal source of frustration to their parents.

The great flood in the year of Hedoterus' birth was indeed a forerunner of a time of prosperity. In succeeding years the floods were equally generous and the brothers pooled their profits to buy their own boat, a graceful, proud craft built by shipwrights of an earlier generation. Nearly a hundred feet long, it rode so lightly on the water that a ballast of sand and stones had to be taken on when the cargo was unloaded. Since a portion of their harvest for some years was committed to pay for the boat, they contracted with neighboring farmers up the river to float their harvests to market more economically than the farmers could do themselves in smaller boats.

The older brother's wife bore him two additional boys in successive years, making a total of five boys with, the proud father boasted, not a girl in the lot. Hedoterus' parents celebrated each birth in the other family with decreasing enthusiasm. His mother, a strong woman not yet twenty-five with good teeth, had no more children despite the fact that she made the arduous journey to the city each year to lay gifts symbolizing the finest of their harvests before the shrines of the fertility gods. After four years she good-naturedly resigned herself to the mysterious displeasure of the gods and devoted herself to the cheerful upbringing of what was to be her only child.

Feeling an irrational guilt because he had produced only one son, Hedoterus' father put the boy to work on the boat with his two older cousins when he was only nine. The mother protested mildly because she would miss him during the long weeks it required to float the more than one hundred miles down the river and be towed back. She was content, however, when she saw how the boy reveled in the life of a boatman. When they acquired more experience, the brothers took their boat all the way to the sea, to Alexandria, to have it fitted with masts and billowing sails with which to ride the winds upriver against the sluggish flow of the river, even against the flood. This enabled them to make two trips each year instead of the customary one.

Young Hedoterus memorized the channels and currents his first trip down the river and thereafter sat proudly if precariously on the once-gilded prow of the boat, shouting directions to the helmsman who manned the huge sweep in the stern. Downriver, they seldom touched shore except to take on cargo from speculators who bought from small farmers but did not deal in sufficient quantities to justify owning or hiring a boat. Living was spartan and tiring going downriver, for the boat must go through the night, with braziers of fragrant cedar burning at the ends of long arms near the prow to warn other craft and give a feeble light on moonless nights.

The prevailing winds came from the sea so the upriver journey was a time for rest, casting fish nets and singing in the night while drinking wine scooped in cups from the earthenware jars which had been so laboriously loaded. Unless they had been delayed at the market within sight of the towering pyramids, there was no night sailing except when the moon reflected silver from the water. By custom they slept on the boat but looked forward to congenial evenings ashore at village taverns where they told extravagant lies of their adventures in the city. Often they carried passengers, mostly farmers encouraged by the good floods who sought to return to their fields which they had left during the dry years.

Hedoterus dozed under a makeshift canopy in the stern, lulled by the soft sound of the wind on the sails and the shushing of the boat's hull through the water. He awoke to the creak of wood as the giant helmsman leaned against the tiller to compensate for a shift in the wind. He studied the helmsman through slitted eyes, wishing he knew more about him. Six and a half feet tall and weighing at least three hundred pounds, the man was bald, his pate burned a deep bronze by the sun. Muscles rippled under the matted graying hair on his bare chest. He had worked this boat under the previous owners but Hedoterus had learned little else about this towering, silent man. When pressed, he would say, "I was born on the river. I will die on the river." This made sense to the young Hedoterus who also loved the river. He felt warm and comfortable near the big man who, with clocklike regularity, spent his entire wages whoring and drinking during the days it took to market the cargo. He somehow always knew when the return sailing was scheduled and would return twelve hours before, bawling lusty songs in an unfamiliar dialect.

A screaming wind-driven rain had forced them to furl their sails and anchor near the shore the day before. The wind was still fitful and low-flying clouds hung overhead but Hedoterus knew they would be home by nightfall. Suddenly the boat heeled far over and river water poured over them. "Drop the sails!" the helmsman bellowed, throwing his strength into the tiller. Before the men could move the wind reversed and blew the sail against the mast. The mast creaked and splintered, then snapped a dozen feet over the deck. Held vertical by the sail which was still secured, the broken butt of the mast plunged down through the deck planking and crunched a hole in the bottom of the boat. Hedoterus' father and cousins ran to the forward mast, slashed the ropes with knives and scampered out of the way as the sail collapsed with a rustling crash. The wind stopped as quickly as it had begun and the boat wallowed as it lost headway, a dead thing in the water.

The sail was cut away from the broken mast but no attempt was made to remove the mast. It had penetrated the bottom of the boat but plugged the hole it had made so that the leakage was not critical. Hedoterus' father scanned the shore, seeking landmarks. "Whose water jurisdiction are we in?"

"We passed Maryeh's pier an hour ago," his brother said, then to the helmsman, "Can you steer us near enough to get a line on?"

The helmsman nodded. "Get the sail out of the water." They looked to the sail, still made fast but dragging the boat in a slow circle as it filled with water and ballooned under the keel.

"Good," the uncle said. "I'll swim to shore and make ready. You should drift there within the next two hours." He tied cords around his trousers at the ankles and dived into the water, taking advantage of the current and swimming with even strokes toward the shore a half mile distant.

The Oriane family furnished Maryeh with much business so Maryeh used all three of his teams of horses to drag the crippled boat onto shore and raise it on a scaffold before sundown. A quick assessment of the damage was made and one of Hedoterus' cousins was sent to walk through the night to bring laborers and supplies the following day. Hedoterus shared a meal of broiled fish with the helmsman, then prepared to skin down the rope to take the bronze platters and cups to the river to wash them. He checked the mooring of the rope tied to the rail, then jumped back, startled. The rope was strained and moved under his hand. Someone else was climbing it.

Sure that everyone was on board and preparing for bed, he dropped his dishes with a clatter and stepped to lean over the rail. As he reached the rail two small hands gripped it, two bare feet swung themselves quickly up and a dark-haired girl jumped to the deck, so close that he had to jump back to prevent her from landing on his feet. "I am Kismé," she said, turning her dark eyes directly to his face for a few seconds, then squinting in the twilight to look over the boat. She turned again to him and he swallowed noisily as he got a second glimpse of her eyes. "Do you have a name?" she said politely.

"I am Hedoterus. My family owns this boat. Are you anything besides Kismé?"

"My father is Maryeh. My family owns the horses and we have this ten-mile water jurisdiction." She appeared impatient. "I am the youngest daughter and Kismé means good-luck-piece in my mother's dialect. Will you show me the boat now, please?"

"It's almost dark," Hedoterus said. "You would be able to see more tomorrow. We will be here several days, until the boat is repaired."

"I want to see it now," she said. "I have seen this boat all my life but when you pass upriver there is either wind for your sails or I am riding another boat."

He leaned closely to see her face. "You ride the boats? A girl?"

"I told you I am the youngest daughter. I am not fit to lead the horses and my family is glad to have me out from underfoot. The river people are kind and offer me food to ride with them. Remember, I am the good-luck-piece." She began walking toward the prow, stepping over the tangled ropes which still littered the deck. She stopped and gazed up at the prow, which seemed more formidable with the boat on the ground with its undersides on the scaffold. "Is that where you ride?" she said. "You were always too far away to recognize."

"Yes. I know the channels and currents better than the others."

"I want to go up there." She jumped to the railing and began to inch her way up the curved prow on her hands and knees. Hedoterus blinked and took a second look at a white, bare behind which showed when her knee-length wrap-around slid up her haunches.

"Not that way," he said urgently. "You straddle it and climb that way. Otherwise you'll fall if the boat dips."

"Silly. The boat's not going to dip on dry land. Besides, there are reasons why I choose not to straddle the thing, as you say."

"So I noticed," he said, under his breath, but she heard him.

"Boys!" she said, exasperated, and flounced her skirt to cover herself, almost toppling off. She recovered her balance and jumped fully eight feet to the deck, landing lightly beside him. She took a final indignant yank at her skirt. "How old are you?"

"Twelve, I think," Hedoterus said. "Why? How old are you?"

"If you're twelve you're too old to be looking up girl's dresses. And I know I'm twelve. A man who works for my father can write and he inscribed my birth date on a bronze tablet with all my brothers and sisters."

Hedoterus was becoming angry. "If you're old enough to worry about things like that, you're old enough to wear pants if you spend most of your time riding boats with men."

She giggled. "I do, but I had to slip out the window to come here and this was the only garment I could find. And why are you angry? I think I have a very nice bottom."

"Then you'd better take your bottom back home before we all get into trouble."

"I will go quietly if you will show me the rest of the boat. This is the most magnificent boat I have ever been on and I must see it all." He could no longer see her face but he knew she had turned her head and was looking at him. "Would I really cause you much trouble if I stayed?"

Embarrassed, he put his hand in the small of her back to guide her. "No, of course not. We have many women and girls who ride with the farmers back upriver." When she felt the pressure of his hand on her back she stiffened, then relaxed and leaned back against him. He wanted to pull away but instead tightened his fingers against the muscles on either side of her spine. "I will have to tell you about what you cannot see." He took his hand away and moved to lead her. She caught his hand as he moved past her and held it fast. He tightened his own grip and moved forward. "Stay near the railing," he said. "Much of the deck planking was taken up to throw out the ballast when we were leaking."

She spoke in a low voice. "It seems unnatural for such a large boat to be out of the water. It was surely not built as a cargo boat. Do you know anything about its history?"

They had circled the deck and Hedoterus drew her into folds of the fallen forward sail, away from the dank wind which blew off the river. "It is said it was built for the pharoah, many years ago, for one of his concubines."

"Do you mean Jeptha?" She laughed. "I understand our phar-oah has little use for women. He is not even married."

Hedoterus shrugged in the dark. "Well, he has no sister to marry, and his mother is dead." He reached to pull the canvas around their legs. "No, this boat was built for the pharoah before Jeptha, long before we were born. It never had sails before my father and uncle had them installed. It was propelled by slaves with oars. Tomorrow I will show you the places where the oars were. They are sealed now so the boat will ride deeper in the water when it is loaded."

They lay for long hours in the nest their body warmth had created in the sail. They didn't speak although each knew the other was awake. She stirred against him. "The wind has blown the clouds away," she said. "The gods promised me there would be stars when I found you." Before he could answer, she went on, "Do you believe in the gods?"

"Uh. . . we're not very religious," he said. "We always make sacrifices to the river gods, of course, and my mother used to say she prayed to the fertility gods until they tired of listening to her."

"Aren't the other boys your brothers?"

"No. Cousins. I am the only child of my parents. But what are you talking about when you say the gods promised you something? Do they talk to you?"

"Sometimes I think they do, inside my head. It's probably just my own head telling me stories. I've always told myself stories because I'm alone so much. I have ten brothers and sisters but none of them like me much."

"Don't your parents care for you?"

"I think my mother does a little but my father doesn't because I'm not a boy. I was very lonely until I started telling myself the stories."

"What kind of stories, especially the one about finding me?" He sat up, letting their cover fall unheeded.

"Oh, I'd see the boat pass downriver with you sitting up there and I'd go to bed and dream about riding up there with you. It seemed like I really was, with the warm wind and the sound of big splashes in the water you can't figure out. I even remember you counting to yourself so you could call to the helmsman when to change course. Why, what's the matter?" she said as she felt a thrill pass from his body where they touched.

"Nobody in the world could have known that," he said in a whisper. "I memorized the currents and channel changes by count-ing my heartbeats. I never told anyone because my father and uncle boasted to everyone that I had 'the gift'. That sounded more exciting than counting so I let them think it."

"A memory like that is a true gift, Hedoterus, although I have ridden with you so many times I wager I could do nearly as well as you."

"But, how could you. . .? I don't understand. . ."

"I don't understand, either. Now cover us again. The wind is cold."

In the morning they scrambled over the boat, Kismé asking endless questions Hedoterus was hard put to answer. At noon they were sharing a leg of lamb Kismé had sneaked from the family kitchen while watching the helmsman strain to remove the butt of the broken mast from the boat's hull without causing further damage. The helmsman stopped to rest, then stepped to them and took one in each huge arm and tossed them up to the deck. Kismé landed lightly, like a cat, and yelled down, "Why did you do that? We weren't bothering you!"

The helmsman didn't look up but wrapped his arms around the mast and with a mighty heave accompanied by the sound of splintering wood, lifted the mast and let it fall exactly where they had been sitting. "Oh," Kismé said.

In the afternoon they were pressed into service sorting and coiling the tangled rope on the deck. Kismé sat with Hedoterus cross-legged on the deck as he showed her how to splice and mend broken rope to where only a practiced eye could see the new fibers woven into the old. As the daughter of their host, Hedoterus' father and uncle treated Kismé with quiet country courtesy, inviting her to share their meals of fish and fried bread and hiding their smiles when Hedoterus boldly dipped a cup of wine and handed it to her with much ceremony. That night they curled up to sleep on woven reed pallets on the deck until a fresh rain drove them below deck where they dried themselves on the rough bags which still smelled warmly of the grain which had been dumped from them a week ago at the market.

The following morning a crude raft was poled along near the shore to Maryeh's pier. The raft was pulled ashore and dismantled; the lumber was now water soaked and would be more pliable when fitted to the curving hull of the boat. When the boat was again hauled out of the river, the new timbers would dry and shrink, binding the seam of the repaired section more tightly in place. Activity began at once, everyone instictively glancing at the sky, hoping for a few days delay before the torrential, blinding rains brought the surface of the river to seething hissing life.

Hedoterus and Kismé were banished from the boat. She took

him to her home, a recently built, solid but crowded house constructed with a high balcony to give a downriver view of boats coming into their jurisdiction which would need the ten-mile upriver tow. One boat was waiting at the pier, another was in sight, being towed to join it. "That means they will be towed together," Kismé explained. "It is slower but my father charges a little less that way." She clapped her hands. "It also means they will use the three-horse team which my older brother always leads. He seems to like me more than the others and, with you along, he may let us ride the horses when we are out of sight of the house."

Kismé's brother offered no objection to them riding when Hedoterus offered to talk about the city he had left only a few days before. "We have horses for our farms," Hedoterus said. "They are not like these. Aren't these the same horses they use in the city for building?"

The man grunted and slapped one of the huge beasts on the shoulder, and Hedoterus sensed he had made a friend. "They are the same breed," the man said. "But these are river horses, not your ordinary city work horses. We buy them when they are very young from the Bedouin breeder in the Great Oasis three days from here."

"What is the difference?" Hedoterus said. "They look the same."

"It is their training," Kismé's brother said. "You have seen them working at building in the city. The horses are harnessed in teams of a dozen or more to a long pole, a ram they call it. The horses are trained to push. This does not use their strongest muscles and they weaken and die young." He ran his hand over the animal's back. "Our horses are trained to pull. This is natural for them. And we never overwork them. This team has been working for over fifteen years and they are still strong for five years or more."

"It is said you have the finest horses on the river

"There are many fine horses, when they are of this breed," the man said, but he was pleased. "I want to breed our own. Maybe with another good year, we can afford to buy good breeding stock. The Bedouins know the value of stallions and sell them dearly."

They reached the next pier and the boats were roped to another waiting team of horses. Kismé and Hedoterus made a dozen trips to the river with leather buckets. They poured them over the sweating horses while Kismé's brother rubbed them down with a rough cloth. The driver of the fresh team watched them and laughed. "You make much over dumb beasts."

"I get much from my dumb beasts," Kismé's brother said. "Your master would do well to learn that."

Repairs were completed on the fourth day, the boat slid down the mud bank to the river and ballast was taken aboard. The helmsman stamped around the craft for an hour inspecting the work, then pronounced it fit to be towed home. Maryeh, the owner of the horses, stood on the pier with Hedoterus' father and uncle while they discussed payment for the services. Maryeh politely insisted that if they would drop off some feed for the horses their next trip downriver it would be more than adequate payment. The Oriane brothers pressed him to also accept gold. Kismé stood behind her father, nervous. When she spoke, the words rushed out. "I will go with them, father. Hedoterus' mother has no daughters to help her in the kitchen and your own eyes will tell you I am not needed here. When I try to help I only get in the way and my older sisters beat me."

Her father, embarrassed, put his hand awkwardly on her head. "A man of property does not send his children into the service of others."

"It will not be as a servant," she said. "Hedoterus can come back here when there is little work there for him. You and the older brother are always complaining that you have too few hands to care for the horses."

Unexpectedly, Maryeh laughed. "I think there is something more than horses between you and young Hedoterus. Don't tell me puppy love has come to my baby! I hadn't realized you'd grown this fast."

Tears came to Kismé's eyes at the first affectionate words she remembered her father speaking to her but she stood firmly and looked into his face. "I never want to leave Hedoterus again," she said with great intensity. "Never!"

Subdued by the child's vehemence but amiable, Maryeh said, "There are other people to be consulted in this, my daughter. I can see you have our young guest helplessly ensnared but I think it would be in keeping with good manners to consult with his family."

Hedoterus' timid father looked to his brother for support but found none. "Ah. .. we have help around the household. Servants, you know. But if it will make my son happy I'm sure the girl could be helpful to my wife. Ah. . . it would be like having another child after all these years. Very good, very good indeed." He stopped and looked appealingly at Maryeh, hoping he would not be expected to say more.

Grateful to each other, the fathers sighed almost in unison. "I thank you for your agreement, Oriane," Maryeh said. "But my child will be a stranger in your neighborhood. By law, I think she needs a seal or document to show she is not a runaway slave. Are there

those in your family who can write? No? Nor in mine, but there is a
scribe who lives a day's ride to the North. I will send for him."

Hedoterus spoke for the first time, to Maryeh. "Sir, does that
mean Kismé may not go with us now?"

Again the man laughed, something deep within him awakening. "No, young man. Take my girl. I will have the document done
and send it upriver with one of the boats we serve. May the gods
watch over you."

Warmed by being addressed as 'young man' instead of the
customary 'hey you', Hedoterus began to walk away with slow
dignity. He broke into an excited laughing run, however, when
Kismé grabbed his hand and led him up the hill to her home to
gather her few belongings.

There was confusion when Kismé arrived at the Oriane house.
The six boys shared sleeping rooms and there was much scurrying
to prepare yet another room for Kismé. The helmsman, however,
solved everyone's problem by erecting a heavy felt-lined tent on
the deck of the boat which had again been drawn nearly a mile
ashore above the expected flood level for completing of repairs.
There was some murmuring when it was learned that Hedoterus
slept most nights there with her but his mother dismissed it with,
"Let the children have their way."

<hr>

A year later Hedoterus returned from three months with
Kismé's family in time to begin the first trip downriver. It was now
obvious to everyone that the 'children' were children no longer.
Kisme's breasts were developing full and round; Hedoterus' voice
had deepened and his sinewy shoulders were broadening. The
boat tied up at Maryeh's pier to unload the grain in payment for last
year's boat repair work. Hedoterus' father sought out Maryeh and
they sat on bags of grain in the stables, sharing a cup of cider. "This
is difficult for me Maryeh. . . Did you know that your daughter and
my son, uh. . . sleep together?"

Maryeh took a pull at his cider. "Haven't they always?"

"Yes, but they're not children anymore. You know what I
mean. . .?"

The older Maryeh hugged the younger man affectionately.
"Friend Oriane, you took my daughter into your home as a member
of your family. Of what concern is it of mine how you manage your
personal family affairs. Wait. I know what you're going to say. When
Hedoterus is here, he is regarded as a member of my family and I

assure you I am far too busy to furrow my brow over the sleeping habits of my family."

"But they should marry, don't you think?"

"I have no objection to that," Maryeh said. "My daughter is of marriageable age and I would consider it an honor to have our families so joined. Do you have some objection?"

"Perhaps I am bound by the habits and traditions of my family but the feeling of my wife and myself is that Hedoterus is too young for this responsibility."

"You are neither an idle talker nor thinker, Oriane. What is it you wish to say?"

Oriane took a deep breath, again thankful for the other man's good nature. "Our family is establishing an agency in the city, so that we may deal more profitably. I propose to place Hedoterus there with two older men to help and, most important, to gain experience. It is to this end that I ask you to release him from his promised duties with you."

"Done!" Maryeh shouted. "Come to the house. We will drink to this with good wine!"

"There is yet another thing which must be understood, Maryeh. Kismé, your daughter, insists on going with Hedoterus and living there with him."

"Do you think it is in our power to separate them? The gods have willed it. Come. I thirst for wine."

Kismé and Hedoterus were found a room large enough for sleeping and cooking over a charcoal brazier. Adulthood was thrust upon them by Hedoterus' long and tedious hours at the counting tables but they found many hours to wander and explore the wonders of the city hand in hand, still children. They were married in a temple when they were not quite fifteen. Hedoterus' conservative father had wished for an additional year but Kismé was very pregnant.

Kismé was delighted to find girls her own age and even younger in the temple who watched the wedding ceremony and then gathered around her, chatting. She had seen them before in the temple gardens; they had smiled and invited her to visit but, shy, she had passed on by. Now she found the girls more excited by her pregnancy than impressed by her marriage, making dozens of offers of help from advice on midwifery to diet. Struck with an idea, Kismé shushed them and said, "My father is here and it would make him proud to take a momento of this day back to our home on the river. Can any of you write?" They answered in chorus; they could all write. Two of them raced each other to a building and returned with a rich sheet of papyrus. After some discussion, the best scribe was brought forward and wrote to Kismé's dictation: "On this day were Hedoterus and his good-luck-piece, Kismé, married in the garden of the temple of the God of the Elements." The girls decided it was very good and ran to find the priest to imprint the seal of his ring on a drop of warm wax. It was Maryeh's finest day.

Walking back to their living quarters, Hedoterus complained, "Why were you so long with the temple girls? I though we'd never get away."

"Are you so anxious to bed down your bride who is seven months pregnant?" She laughed at him, squeezing his arm. "Oh, it's just so different. I thought the temple was all ritual and discipline and long faces."

"I'm glad you made new friends," he said, warming to see her so happy.

"Oh, yes!" She stopped him in the street. "They say I can even go there to have my baby. They have midwives and doctors and a clean hospital."

"We can't afford such frills as that."

"We pay only what we afford to pay, or nothing. Because we were married in the temple of the God of the Elements we are under his protection and that means. . ." Her voice trailed off. "I'm not really sure what it does mean. You will let me return, though, won't you? Just to visit?"

He put his arm around her shoulders and urged her on, smiling. They walked another quarter hour in silence. She slipped an arm around his waist. "Hedoterus. . .?"

"If it's more about the temple, it can wait. We must hurry to say goodbye to our families before the boat sails."

"Just one more thing. We won't even have to stop walking."

"All right."

"They, the girls there, say they can teach me to write and to read."

He stopped this time, as if a wall of brick had fallen in front of him. "Write and read? You? Whatever in the world for?"

"Why shouldn't I? Wouldn't you like to be able to read and write?"

"I can read cargo manifests, accounting records and am very good at figures. What more could I possibly want or need?"

"I'm not sure," she said. "I must think more about it. But come. You are the one delaying now. I must stop first at our house and get the new bridle I plaited for my older brother's riding horse."

Hedoterus resisted Kismé's request to stay at the temple during the last two weeks of her pregnancy. . . until false (and perhaps faked) labor pains sent him on a futile and frustrating search for a sedan chair in the middle of the night. He was welcome to visit her at all times but was self-conscious and seldom stayed long. When the day came one of the girls ran across the city to tell him the time was near but when he arrived an hour later he found he was already the father of a healthy baby girl. Silently outraged because his first born was not a boy, he only half listened to his young wife's account of how she had been trained in natural hypnosis until the birth was almost painless. Full awareness came to him when she took the tiny bundle from her breast and handed it to him. He looked into the little face with its eyes pinched shut and was awed by the feeble pawing of the minute hands and arms. Life! A new life! And it was his, and hers! Hedoterus wept as he knelt to kiss his wife's cheek.

It was more than five years later and after the birth of their third child before Hedoterus could enter the temple without a vague feeling of embarrassment. With a singleness of purpose which sometimes annoyed him, Kismé had become a voracious reader although her writing seldom earned more than an acceptable nod from the priests and priestesses who recognized the girl's intelligence and helped her whenever their duties permitted. They now loaned her valuable scrolls which she took home and read to Hedoterus at night.

She was by this time more adept at bargaining and bookkeeping than he so had stayed behind at the agency. He entered the temple alone with scrolls under his arm she had promised to return that day. He found the priest who was keeper of the archives, returned the scrolls and accepted the priest's invitation to sit with him in the garden. "We see too little of you, Hedoterus," the priest said. "It is a pity you come as a messenger and not as a seeker of learning." He indicated the scrolls which lay on the bench.

"You mean because I have never learned to read." Hedoterus closed his eyes and began to recite in a dreamy voice. "And the people turned from the priests and the holy places and began to build altars and high towers of their own. The unification of the multitudes directed toward gods of their own creation resulted in a discordant dissonance reflecting adversely against the spiritual-magnetic field shrouding this planet. As the spirit of rebellion rose in the people, the counter forces arose, not as punishment but to protect themselves against a rampant surge of self-will which, if unchecked, would spread throughout the universe. As the wills of the people rose in obstinance, so did the waters of the planet rise as the combined forces of resistance buffeted the magnetic guidance and swung the planet on its axis. The enlightened built great boats and provisioned them, far inland. During the final days the mountains rent themselves as wombs and gave birth to liquid fire which burned the land until it sank beneath the sea. The enlightened obeyed the whims of the winds and waves aboard their great boats and as the strongest survived, came to rest on these shores."

The priest's mouth hung open. "You memorized that!"

"Night before last, as Kismé read it to me," Hedoterus said casually. "I know them all. This one appealed to me especially."

"Do you have comprehension. . . do you understand what it says?"

Hedoterus shrugged. "In a general way. Mostly, I just like the sound of the words."

"That's the most fabulous memory I've ever seen! How do you do it?"

Self-conscious, Hedoterus ducked his head. "I don't 'do' anything. I just remember everything that happens. It came to me on the river, when I memorized the channels and currents. I am also good with figures and accounting in my head but Kismé says businessmen believe only what they see written on papyrus or clay tablets. I suppose she's right."

"You have a gift of the gods," the priest said in a reverant voice. "Have you any idea how valuable you could be to us, here in the temple?"

Hedoterus laughed, genuinely amused. "Forgive me, but I have little interest in learning and things spiritual. One in the family is enough."

"Yes, your Kismé is a remarkable young woman. The novices adore her and several of them spend most of their free hours copying scrolls for her." The priest spread his hands apologetically. "I fear she will never be an accomplished scribe."

"There is no need," Hedoterus said. "We will be leaving soon. I miss being on the river."

"You don't mean you're going back to living on a boat?"

"Well, yes, we will. I will be the master of it, though. Various merchants have pooled their money and bought a boat almost as large as that of my family. Hopefully, I will become a floating merchant. We will take copperware and bronze, woven linens, spices, what-have-you upriver and trade them for hardwood, wool, fur with which to make felt. . ."

The priest shook his head. "You will have to go very far upriver for those products."

"We intend to. We will go upriver as far as we can in the summer and return with the flood. We will be going when the river subsides. Thank you for your many kindnesses to my wife." He grasped the priest's hand and walked from the garden.

The boat put under Hedoterus' command had been a sea-going vessel, not as graceful or swift as his family's boat but more stable in the water. It had been built with passable living quarters forward for the captain and his family and walled sleeping room below decks for the crew. Hedoterus chose to move his boat upriver by horse tows for the nearly two hundred miles where they were available. It was the season when long waits at the piers were common. Runners were hired to precede the boat with word that a new merchant ship was enroute. People were invited on board to shop and to ride the ten miles to the next pier if they wished. The first trip brought more curiosity seekers than buyers but by the second year the merchant ship did so well that it traveled empty, completely sold out, during the last week to its final destination to load the valuable hardwood logs which would be turned to floors and furnishings by craftsmen in the city.

The merchants who owned Hedoterus' boat became rich and bought other boats. Hedoterus indifferently declined an offer for a minor partnership in the enterprise and was content when an agreement was sealed making him lifetime proprietor of the boat he operated. Kismé was less content for a few years until she noticed the strength, peace and dignity their children were grow-ing into as compared to the crawling, thieving mass of city children who frequented the market area where they were obliged to spend several weeks each year. She spent this time with her children at the temple, sending them to those eager to teach while she charm-ed the temple scribes into copying more scrolls for her which she in turn drilled into her children during the long months on the river.

When her duties to her children and Hedoterus' responsi-bilities to the boat could be relaxed, they spent long evenings together on the sheltered deck above their cabins. Then she would talk, long monologues which appeared to be directed to the winds but which she knew were being absorbed by the amazingly reten-tive but unambitious mind of her mate.

In some way she did not understand, it rested him while refuel-ing some vital forces within him. Occasionally he would respond and they would spend long dreamy nights in slow conversation. On one such night, when their oldest daughter had caused an embarrassing, shouting scene, she said, "Our daughter is feeling the urgency of her womb."

"Yes," he agreed. "She should marry. She is nearly fifteen."

"My youngest brother would marry her," Kismé said. "He tells me he has been waiting this full year."

"But he is a man twice her age."

"He is but a year older than I am. Does that make him so very ancient?" she said, the amusement in her voice causing him to remain silent. "And he is a good river man. As my father has often said, may the gods forgive me, he is no good with horses. And there is room to build them an apartment, Hedoterus. . . there, amidships where the main mast was taken out when this boat was taken from the sea."

"Yes," he said. "That has been in my mind."

"Good. When the builders are aboard it will be a good time to roof and seal this place where we are sitting so we can also sleep here in all weather. The temple architect made me scale drawings for such an addition the last time we were in the city."

He drew a deep breath with which to launch the tirade which welled up within him. She settled herself more comfortably against him, waiting. He let his breath out and tightened his arm around her, stroking her breast in the gentle way he knew she liked. "You have bewitched me, woman. From the very first day."

"I remember," she said. "Didn't you really recognize me then?"

"No," he said shortly. "I will still have nothing to do with this spirit nonsense of yours, that we have lived other lifetimes together and that we planned to mate in this one. It's a good thing I got you out of the temple when I did. They would have ruined you."

"Then why do you permit me and the children to go there when we are in the city?"

"Because it pleases you. It flatters my maleness to please you." They didn't speak for some minutes. He lifted her face and kissed her on the mouth. "Dear love, I only know that we are one person. I recognize that you are stronger, more aggressive and more intelligent than I am. I know that in some way I will never understand we are a part of each other. Somehow through you I have learned to accept the death that must come to us all. I am not hurrying toward it, but I do not dread it. I will not ask because I know you will not tell me, but I am sure you know when our allotted span will end." He stopped, abashed at the formal words he had been using. "I am not good with words."

"You are very good, with many things," she whispered. "When the builders have completed our new bedroom here you will again be able to demonstrate them."

"You are totally depraved." He slapped her sharply on the rump, which made her squeal. Laughing softly and holding hands to guide each other down the ladder quietly so they would not awaken the children, they descended to their own sleeping pad.

———————◁ ▷———————

The trials of the river were many. Their first grandchild was born dead when the mother fell from her bunk an hour before she delivered the child and hurt herself when the boat tilted during a tricky docking maneuver. Kismé screamed and cursed the boat and stayed ashore with a family in the steamy upriver jungle for an entire half year. Lonely and hurt, Hedoterus took a village girl downriver and into his bed. He knew the dark-skinned girl was being sent by her improverished family to the city to become a prostitute but he underestimated her preliminary training until she disappeared into the city with half his accumulated year's profit of gold. He used the other half to hire an effeminate decorator to ride upriver with him and decorate his living cabin extravagantly with imported silks and scented fabrics.

Kismé returned to the boat, gladly and penitently. She immediately sensed the guilt motivation behind the elaborate decor but said nothing. During the month they spent in the humid upriver jungle climate the finery mildewed and rotted and was thrown overboard, along with the decorator who called the curses of every god he knew upon their heads as he swam to shore. When they again embraced it was on resilient reed mattresses held in a bed frame of hand-woven ropes.

They were saddened as the oldest girl took her husband from the boat and settled in a growing upriver community. Kismé took her private joy when her daughter took the treasured scrolls and began to teach the rudiments of reading and writing to the children in the village where she and her husband had settled. The younger children, another girl and a boy, melted into the city.

By this time they had enured themselves against the breaking of the traditional family ties of the river and farm people, accepting the acceleration of the more modern and enlightened generation. They were perplexed and depressed when the other daughter contracted and died agonizingly of syphilis but they took heartening joy together when their only son was admitted to a temple as a novice. Kismé fretted because the temple was more liberal and not dedicated to any particular god, but was comforted when their son ultimately took the vow of silence which would lead to his initiation into rites his parents had only vaguely dreamed about.

And the river was good to them. In the city, Hedoterus complained that his 'elbows were tied to his sides'. Kismé thrived on the vitality of the city until the death of their younger daughter, after which she seldom left the boat when it was there except for her visits to the temple. Once, when Hedoterus was glowing with wine, she persuaded him to recite from his memory of the scrolls to the dozen or so passengers they were carrying upriver. He soon overcame his shyness and 'read' whenever he had an audience. Under bemused protest, he also read to the black people far upriver. They did not understand the language he spoke but enjoyed the sound of his voice so much they squatted in patient silence until he became hoarse.

His first reaction when Kismé became ill with an unknown fever in the upriver jungle was indignation. It was true they had lived more than fifty years, longer than most, but they were river people and as such were under the special protection of the river gods. Their faces were lined and darkened by countless thousands of hours in the sun but they were strong and responded with lusty enjoyment to life as it came to them. She weakened but seemed to revive when they neared the village where their oldest daughter had settled. Reasonably claiming she wanted to spend a few weeks with their grandchildren, she persuaded Hedoterus to continue downriver and back without her.

It was not until he was a day's journey away from her that it came to him that this was the first time they had been separated for twenty years. He grouched through the journey, made impossible demands of his crew and sold his cargo at a substantial loss. He paid the exorbitant fees to have his boat night-towed upriver to rejoin his wife. He fumed when he awoke on the final day to find a line of boats ahead of him awaiting the next tow; it would be another half day before he could tie up at the pier. He grudgingly allowed his sullen crew to take the small boat and row upstream to the village. He was surprised an hour later to see the boat returning with two oarsmen and a passenger. His heart lifted when he saw the passenger was a woman but sank in dread when he saw it was his daughter.

His daughter threw herself over the railing and ran into his arms. "What is it, child? Where is your mother?" He was not aware that he was shouting.

His daughter held him for a moment longer, and he knew before she said the words. "She is dead, father. It was last week."

"What happened? She wasn't that ill."

His daughter let him lead her into the shelter of the midship apartment which had been her home when she and her husband had lived with her parents on the boat. "We didn't think so, either, father. Eight days ago she said she was tired and went to bed early, before dinner. She had done this before. The next morning I sent the children to her with breakfast. . . and she was dead."

He exhaled a deep breath and appeared to grow smaller. "You buried her? Of course. Take me there."

Hedoterus interrupted his upriver trip only long enough to spend a night-long vigil by his wife's grave. The remainder of the journey went according to schedule, with the crew muted and cooperative, obscurely ashamed of their earlier anger at the master's harshness during the downriver run. By rare good fortune Hedoterus was able to purchase a full cargo of ebony logs brought from the far interior of the continent. The crew was jubilant and even Hedoterus appeared to shed his grief. With a full cargo they could go downriver under sail without the customary stops and would arrive in the city perhaps ten days earlier than usual. They also knew that ebony was worth almost its weight in silver and were elated when the master told them he would share a portion of this extra windfall with them.

His employers had not expected him to return so early so the merchandise for his next river trip was not yet assembled. Leaving his boat at anchor, he wandered again through the city as he had done with Kismé so many years before. He stopped to chat at length with friends, spent a dull but relaxed day with his son who was now a full initiate in the temple priesthood. . . but he avoided the temple where his Kismé had been such an eager student. At the end of a week he brought his boat to the pier to supervise the loading. As was his custom, he took the dangerous job of standing in the boat's hold to guide the placing of the heavier part of the load. A ton of solid brass cookware packed into a net swung over his head. He stood to one side until it was positioned as he wanted , then stepped directly underneath. "Slowly, men, slowly!" he yelled. "We don't draw wages for damaged wares!"

"HEDOTERUS!" a crewman screamed. "The line is parting! Get out of the way!"

Above, the rope as thick as a man's arm which held the net quivered with strain. A single strand broke and the ends curled into themselves. Another strand broke, then a handfull. "Get out, Hedoterus! Get out!" Tantalizingly, the net held for a second longer on a single strand, then fell with a jangling crash to the bottom of the boat. A cloud of dust rose as men rushed to tear at the tumbled metal. One man glanced at the man beside him and stopped working. The others stopped. "Why didn't he get out of the way? He had plenty of time," one said.

"We'll never know," another said, as they began to pass the brass from hand to hand to uncover the mangled body underneath.

Another, who had counted Hedoterus' heartbeats during this final trip downriver, knew.

Kismé knew.

It's an unscholarly way to do things but, as I mentioned earlier, any research for background material was done after each lifetime was written up. Although we found no wild discrepancies between the information we received psychically and that which we got later from reading up on the probable historical periods of the stories, advance research could have colored the initial writing.

When I sat Keetoowah down and asked him if he recognized himself as a Nile river man, he looked at me over his glasses and said, "What do you think?" I just nodded while I marveled at the striking physical similarities between my friend of today and the powerful helmsman on the boat where Hedoterus spent his boyhood. The bald pate, muscle-bunched shoulders and sun-bronzed skin would cause a second look, now or three thousand years ago.

I hadn't paid much attention while writing of the roistering helmsman. I had warm and ancient memory of a companionable, silent man of uncertain origin and background who had cared enough to make a young boy feel comfortable in an adult world. Realizing who he had been, I wanted to find out more about him. I almost wish I hadn't.

Inducing a meditative trance, I channeled my basic recall to his vibrations and returned in spirit to join my friend during his last days in Egypt. It wasn't a happy story and still brings pain so I will abbreviate it to its essence. The big man stayed with the Oriane family boat until after Hedoterus and Kismé were settled in what is now Cairo. During one monumental binge between trips he fell into a drunken camaraderie with a contingent of Roman legionnaires. He awoke the next day chained to a galley oar far from land, enroute to Italy. He ended his days as a slave in Rome. I felt an involuntary remorse because I had never even learned his name. He was called "Talus", the vernacular of the time for 'mine worker'. The only reference he made to his past was an occasional obscure remark about part of his young manhood spent 'in the underground' deep in the African interior.

We had a near-miss not long ago which almost gave us an extended close-up look at present day Egypt. A close friend I'll call Mac had lived in Egypt, married to an Egyptian woman. When he was divorced he learned that although he was free to leave the country a considerable fortune on deposit in Egyptian banks was impounded. He could spend it any way he chose as long as he didn't try to take it out of the country.

Mac was good naturedly lamenting this state of affairs one evening when Carol, naturally enough, began to question him about Egypt. I had just given Mac a quickie life reading which had traced a puzzling physical disorder to a past lifetime. I was still in a mild haze, the usual after-images tumbling through my mind, only half listening to the conversation. The repeated questions about Egypt penetrated to a critical area of my semi-awareness and I suddenly flashed on the Nile river and how it was thousands of years ago. I startled Mac with a sharp question: "Do the river people still use those heavy wooden boats with the big triangular sails?" Yes, he said. He understood the traditional craft of boat building had remained virtually unchanged throughout history.

This opened up a new conversational avenue which began to shape into a plan over the following few weeks. Mac decided that by golly, if he couldn't get his money out of Egypt we'd all pack up, go to Egypt and spend it! We had a lot of fun making plans even though we all, including Mac, knew he was dying of cancer. We just didn't know how fast he was dying. Mac didn't make it back to Egypt. Nor did we.

Vivid Egyptian memories were awakened a final time when we visited the King Tutankhamen exhibit which toured the United States. As soon as we entered the museum I felt what can only be described as a high intensity buzzing which excited me so much I almost bounced out of my wheel chair. Another museum visitor was reading aloud from the guide booklet we'd bought at the door. And I was saying to Carol, "Oh no, that's not the way it was at all. . . those alabaster vases were carved while completely immersed in water. And another thing. . ." I must have lectured until I was hoarse; we were in the museum for hours while I completely lost myself in fast-moving visualizations of life as it was lived in the time of Tutankhamen, the boy king whose funeral relics have had such an impact on modern thinking.

My pleasure in this happening was heightened because the King Tut artifacts were of the same general era as the time we spent a lifetime on the Nile river. The biggest thrill was seeing a gilded replica of one of the royal barges. It was somewhat different from the big craft on which Hedoterus had spent his boyhood but I centered my eyes on the upraised prow. I forgot the penetrating chill of the air conditioned museum and inhaled again the fetid odor of the mud banks of the river baking in the sun. I felt the power of the water as it pulled the boat downstream and the often choppy plunging as the current contested the propulsion of the wind-filled sails on the long upstream journey. I was once more limp with the heat, drawing buckets of river water up to dribble over my head and luxuriating as the evaporation cooled my skin for a few minutes. I recalled the gnawing tenseness of shivering while trying to stay awake at night to call the channels during the marathon down-river runs. I was there again and, although I had a twinge of nostalgia, I was secure enough in my present creature comforts to be glad I wouldn't have to do it again.

VI

One of the most pathetic of the astral forms is the spirit which finds itself earthbound and can't figure out what to do about it. Some are trapped in this nebulous limbo by their own guilt and remorse, as was Carol's husband. Most, however, are caught there because they don't know they're dead. They awaken following illness or accident in familiar surroundings, in a materially solid form, still able to see their friends and loved ones, and usually maddeningly frustrated because nobody will pay any attention to them. The chances are they remember details of their final mortal days but if they're still in the same locale and still have substance, they just can't be dead! Invariably they seem to be people who feared physical death and made no preparation for the one event none of us escapes. If they allowed the thought of death to enter their minds at all, they probably dismissed it with some absurdity such as visualizing themselves as some ethereal, wispy floating thing. Or they forsaw oblivion. Which I admit could be terrifying. Of course, there are always spirits on that side to meet them but, they reason, of what use are spirits if I'm not dead?

One particularly appealing incident comes to mind. Before I met Carol on this plane, I shared an old house in Denver with a grown son. He's a psychically sensitive lad and shortly after moving in with me began to insist that someone else was in his room with him late at night. I checked it out and we agreed there was a barely visible something in one corner of the room. But I could make no contact with whatever it was, and this puzzled me. It is not unusual for an earthbound spirit to manifest itself visually, as witnessed by the countless 'ghost' sightings by credible people. They have even frequently been photographed. Within my own experience, though, I have found that these spirits are seldom telepathic; it is usually necessary to converse with them verbally and receive their answers telepathically, although they think they are actually talking and being heard.

My son Danny and I persisted because whatever was in his room was obviously deeply troubled. We enlisted the aid of psychic friends and eventually, painstakingly came to know Nan. Nan had died in that room when she was seventeen years old and the poor thing had been hovering around there, all alone, for fifty-four years. The reason she had not been able to respond to us at the outset was because she had forgotten how to talk. I immediately released her to the loving custody of Pa, that wonderful man whose spirit is always there when needed.

Danny and I were happy for Nan, and just a little glad to have her out of the house. But she came bounding back within twenty-four hours, happy as a sunbeam and spraying love in all directions. I asked her then if there hadn't been spirits who had come for her after her physical death. Of yes, she said, but she was afraid of ghosts and ran away! Although no longer earthbound, Nan stayed with us until Danny went to make his home in Europe, and went with him. He has written of a couple of impish tricks she has pulled on him so I'm reassured that little Nan is, finally, thoroughly enjoying life.

There are yet other entities who eased from this life form to the next without the befuddlement of going through an earthbound phase but are still unhappy about the whole affair. I have read a good deal in support of the theory that many of our present day young social dissidents are the angry spirits of young soldiers whose earthly lives were cut short in a war they neither inaugurated nor abetted. I survived a couple of wars within the period of a dozen years, one of them in a noncombatant status, and I saw a lot of dead young men. I was a young man during the period of 1941 to 1945 and I most emphatically didn't want to be dead, but a number of other young men in the German army tried earnestly to kill me, and very nearly succeeded a couple of times. I have never had personal contact with any of these spirits of dead boy-soldiers but suspect I might very well be angry were I numbered among them.

Other spirits, many whose earthly beliefs were founded on fundamentalist Christianity, arrive on the other side and discover there are no pearly gates through which to pass, no streets paved with gold. There are no angels swooping around twanging on harps and God is not sitting on a throne of clouds stroking His beard. These souls have not developed, in any lifetime, sufficiently to achieve the beginnings of true Spirituality (which, in all humility, I submit as being the ultimate purpose of the infinite God) and they are downright miffed to find their narrow expectations unsupported in material fact. They withdraw into themselves or with others of their kind and sulk. Or the equivalent of sulking; they decline to make any effort to improve their lot by sending their love to troubled souls still on earth, by receiving and comforting new arrivals, or any of the countless ways certainly open to them. Surely those souls are deserving of our most earnest prayers.

Shortly after Carol and I were married Joe, an older son asked us to attempt to contact Jake, a contemporary of his who had died the year before. Jake was about 18 at the time. I made contact with him although the nature of the communication leads me to believe it wasn't a 'direct' -- Jake wasn't an adept at contacting those on this plane, and communicated first-person through someone else who was. This happens frequently and I like to think that certain spirits assign themselves to this useful duty.

Jake wasn't happy. He had died of illness, growing progressively weaker, so his passing had not been a shock and he had apparently been received without trauma. But he was bitter about having gone so young, about missing what he still thought of as the good life with his buddies, although our son assured him it wasn't all that great. Jake wanted, in his nostalgia, to reincarnate to rejoin his friends but realized, in his words, "All you guys will be old bastards then." His complaint of his present existence was typical of that voiced in chorus everyday across the world, "They're all too square!"

Neither Carol nor I found that unreasonable; we've even been moved to say the same thing about some of our own kids. But didn't Jake know he could create any environment he wanted there? No, he didn't know that, didn't know how. He was just wandering around, lost. We broke off for a family debate -- what had he enjoyed most while living on earth? Our son Joe said Jake had been a pretty good guitar player but had only been able to afford a cheap, nylon-stringed instrument. This was at least something to go on, so I got back to Jake and asked how'd he like to have a guitar where he is. Coming alive now, he said, "Great! A 12-string?" I told Joe to concentrate on the best 12-string he could imagine, in every detail. We weren't at all sure of what we were doing nor did we have the foggiest notion that we were doing it right. But we wanted, with all our hearts, for this lonely youngster to have that 12-string guitar.

After considerable concentration, I still had no idea whether we were making any forward progress or not. Then, as if in answer to our prayer, I received a fantastic visual image of what could be described only as a real gone, spaced-out cat who had created himself an enormous mountain where he sat, all alone, playing an exotic guitar of his own design. We called this character to Jake's locale. The hilltop guitar-player never identified himself but the communication ceased immediately and I had a fleeting image of the two of them wandering off in the direction of that fabulous mountain, playing their guitars. A precautionary note would be appropriate here: I'm sure we had nothing to do with 'creating' Jake's guitar although we did have something to do with bringing him together with someone who could show him how to do it. I mention this because we will not entertain requests for future celestial guitar-making.

Since her interest in the psychic was first aroused, Carol had convinced herself that at one time she must have been an Indian princess, a high priestess or something else equally exalted. When we came together and spirit contact became almost as simple as dialing a telephone, that was one of her first requests, where and when had she been a member of the local royalty? The answer came back from every source: she never had been.

In the introduction to the previous chapter we related the capsule report of the many lives we had had in early Egypt given us by the Poet. In all except the one we finally wrote about we were wealthy and possibly aristocratic. Carol's conviction that she was once a priestess was no doubt a deeply buried memory of desparately, selfishly wanting to be one. In point of fact, I was once a priest in an Egyptian temple. Not a very important one and attained it through an accident of birth rather than by any particular ability in that direction. I evidently shared her ambitions for earthly power, a recurring weakness it has taken a long, long time to overcome. We were obviously aware of this weakness, among others, which led to the almost countless reincarnations. The new incarnations, however, left us wide open for further error and karma which we had to return and try to work off, a veritable treadmill lasting thousands of years.

We didn't ask the Poet about this, but we feel he may have dictated the history of the Tibetan lifetime which follows as a consolation prize for Carol. She was almost a priestess that time.

———◁▷——

In the land in the Himalayas so high it never knows the touch of summer, a child was born. Due to the wealth and high rank of the family a medical lama was in attendance, but his presence was not necessary. He knew, as did the mother, the day the child would be born and his ministrations could have some effect on the child's hour of birth to assure the closest harmony with the preliminary charts already cast by the astrologers. Both the lama and the mother were rather indifferent about the latter. They knew it would be a girl child and as such could not hope to aspire to the highest of the lamastic orders. Indeed, outlying lamasaries were beginning to adopt vows of celibacy. Whether through reasons of religious fervor or a shortage of women was a subject much discussed within the city of Lhasa.

Under slight, relaxing hypnosis from the medical lama, the mother birthed her child as easily as digesting a meal. The infant was placed to its mother's breast for nourishment while the lama's assistant gently bathed both mother and child. The lama beckoned to a teenage girl. "You are this woman's handmaiden? Good. Make ready to take the child to the temple."

The girl was timid and unused to going out at night. "Honorable Medical Lama, the immersion does not take place until morning. The way to the temple is long and filled with danger. Could we not wait until after it is light?"

The medical lama saw her thoughts and smiled. "No harm will come to you, child. The High Lama will be in the temple awaiting you. He must make the telepathic recording of the infant's birth experience. We would not disappoint the High Lama, would we?"

"Forgive my impertience, Honorable Sir," the girl answered, then wrapped the baby in a blanket of yak's wool and left the house. At the temple she had to wait long before surrendering the baby to an attendant. Weary and cold, she found a protected corner, curled herself into a ball and slept. She awoke in full daylight, the bleak sunlight streaming into the unglazed window near where she had slept. In panic, she ran along the passageway the attendant had taken the night before. She stopped an old man in the robe of a serving monk. "Has the immersion of my mistress' baby taken place?" she said, breathless. "I slept because I was tired and cold."

The old monk started, then looked over her head until she began to tremble. Seeming to make a decision, he turned down the corridor. "Follow me," he said, not looking back. "The infant is alive. You may take it home now." The girl shuddered as she took the baby, thankful that she had been born to the serving caste. No child of hers would ever be taken at birth and immersed in icy water to prove its toughness. . . or lack of it. . . so that it would be able to later survive the austere training essential for all marked even before birth for temple life. "The child's name is Sutra-Scanore," the monk said. "Can you remember that or must I waste precious paper to write it out for you?"

"I will remember, Sir," the girl said, and left the temple, wondering what she would say if asked if she had been present at the immersion.

The girl's worries were needless. When she returned to the big house she was instructed to take the baby Sutra-Scanore to the nursery. Except for birthdays, religious festivals and times when important personages visited the house, Sutra-Scanore's mother exhibited a total indifference to her child. Her preliminary training, which was rigorous and joyless, was left in the hands of those who were retained for that purpose. Sutra-Scanore's one importance to the family was that she be adequately prepared to enter the temple service. Two older brothers had been turned out as unfit during their first year in the lamasary so it was essential for the social standing of the family that one child take religious orders. . . even though it had to be a female.

Isolated by wealth and the severe intensity of her training, Sutra-Scanore did not feel bereft of a normal childhood. She often questioned being forced to learn that for which no reason could be given and attained more a detente than rapport with her instructors. Her mind was quick and retentive and she mastered the endless litanies and ceremonies which would be expected of her as a minor priestess. If she showed little religious dedication, her teachers were nonetheless placated by her letter-perfect memorization.

She entered the temple alone on the evening of her fifteenth birthday, weary beyond endurance at having been made to perform intricate passages of her ceremonies for her foolish mother and guests who had gorged themselves to nausea. As instructed, she sat in the lotus position before the doors of the temple until she should be bidden to enter. Although cold, she welcomed the temporary luxury of being completely alone for the first time in her life. Even at home there had been an irritable crone too old for temple duty who had shared her sleeping room to ensure there was no relaxation of body discipline, even while sleeping.

She had fallen effortlessly asleep while sitting when she felt a hand touch her shoulder. "Come inside," a voice said. "I am sorry you had to wait but there have been many visitors filled with empty questions today." She stood and bowed without looking up. "You don't bow to me. I'm only a glorified servant." She looked then, into a friendly young face under a shaven head. Despite her training and repeated instructions to remain impassive under all circumstances, she could not resist answering the smile on the young monk's face.

"I do not know what I am supposed to do now," she said.

"That is my job, to tell you. I welcome all visitors and newcomers. Do you wish to eat?"

"I have eaten my fill, thank you." She stopped and looked closely into his face in the flickering light of a lamp. "Where are you taking me?"

"To the place where you are to sleep. I will show you where you will eat, too. You will be permitted to do much as you please until time to prepare you for your initiation ceremony. You need not attend the services unless you want."

"But I thought I was ready for the initiation," she said impatiently. "I've spent my entire life preparing for it."

He smiled down at her and urged her on with a light pressure on her elbow. "You will have a period of directed meditation while the records are consulted. And please don't ask me about the initiation. I am only a chela and am forbidden access to the Inner Knowledge."

He took her to a small room in a separate wing of the temple and pulled the woolen curtain aside for her to enter. "It's rather small, isn't it?" she said, looking in at the cubicle which seemed crowded with the single low square table. There was neither bed nor chairs.

"This is only temporary. Your quarters after your initiation will be more in keeping with your station." He gave her a quick smile. "I only say what I have heard. No men are allowed there."

"But will I see you again. . . I mean before the initiation?" she said, then looked down, feeling her face grow red.

"I am perhaps the most-seen person in this temple. You will tire of me before long. But if you need me, ask anyone. My name is Manoa-Ulmy. I must leave you now. I want to eat before the evening service." He gave her another smile and was gone, long legs moving him swiftly down the corridor, his worn robe flapping around his ankles.

She did not see Manoa-Ulmy until three days later as she walked along a rooftop to work out the stiffness of a morning-long meditation session. Leaning on the parapet overlooking the city, he did not see her until she came to stand beside him. "So this is why I don't see you," she said. "You hide on rooftops."

"Don't you agree it's a good place?" he said. "Not many come here. A young acolyte was blown to his death a few months ago and that memory is still too fresh in most minds. What have you been doing?"

She made a wry face. "Meditating for four hours every morning and being bored the rest of the day."

"I should think the meditating would be the more boring. To me it always was."

"Oh no. This is the first time in my life I've ever been left alone and I enjoy it." She leaned beside him, their elbows almost touching. "What do you mean, meditation used to bore you?"

"Until three years ago, I was in training over there," he said, pointing to a large lamasary atop a hill several miles distant.

"Isn't that where the medical lamas train? I hear they're very strict there. Is that why you left?"

He laughed. "The discipline didn't bother me. I spent almost half my life there. I entered when I was eight. No, I was very sorrowfully asked to leave because the Lord Abbott didn't think I was serious enough to be a medical lama."

"But what did you do?"

"Nothing very dreadful. I just insisted on enjoying myself while in the midst of those who find no joy in religious life. I was disappointed at being turned out but this is also a good life. I can visit my family whenever I wish and with my training I am a teacher of sorts to the younger boys here. The only thing I dislike is trying to act important to unimportant visitors who in their turn are trying to make me think they are important."

She laughed with him. "This is good, to laugh. I didn't think I knew how. But wait, with all your schooling you must surely know something about what is to happen to me."

"Nothing is going to 'happen' to you. You will just be put with experienced priestesses and shown the duties expected of you, most probably in the services for the dead."

She shuddered. "That seems like a gloomy way to spend a lifetime."

"Not at all," he said, serious. "It's very satisfying to find earthbound spirits and guide them to peace. Women arc often used in this because it is believed by many that lost spirits respond more readily to the voice of a woman."

"And what do you believe?"

"I have no opinion because I have never been present when a priestess was at work."

"But you do have great skill in avoiding leading questions," she sniffed.

"And you have a great deal of curiosity for a novice priestess. I can imagine many days when your teachers had their hands full."

"They did at that," she said, her eyes catching fire. "When do I start? At least you can tell me that much."

"It might be several weeks. To be consecrated your birth record must be at hand and it may take a while to find a fifteen-year-old document. Our library system is not the best here. And then you must have a new horoscope cast to determine the best time for the consecration. And finally, nothing, absolutely nothing is done in a hurry in Tibet. It's the unspoken law of the land."

"I will reconcile myself." She breathed an exaggerated sigh. "Tell me, Manoa-Ulmy, is your family wealthy, too?"

"No. My father is a trader in wool. We were very poor when I was a child. which is why I was made to become a monk, as were two brothers. My father is more successful now and the family is comfortable."

"I had two brothers who were turned out of the temple."

"You had two brothers? Aren't they still your brothers?" He turned to smile at her.

"No. They were not permitted to return to the family after leaving the temple. It was a great disgrace." She ran a forefinger along the stone in front of her. "I don't think I like my family very much. I don't want to talk about them. Tell me about your family, Manoa-Ulmy."

"There is love in my family," he said. She jabbed the stone with her finger in momentary petulance, thinking him rude, wanting to know more. Then with rare wisdom she realized he had said it all. As tears stung her eyes she knew she could not talk to this young man about love because she had never experienced it. But she was to learn. . .

———————⊃ ⊂———

The days became weeks and Sutra-Scanore sulked through her morning meditations, her life bearable only because in the afternoons she might meet Manoa-Ulmy on the rooftop. Often he was busy and did not come, at other times the wind was too fierce to dare exposure to the outside. On these days she wandered the dimly lit corridors, often stopping in a deserted chapel to practice her litanies, as she had been told she could do. She would invariably ask Manoa-Ulmy for news of her consecration and he would always shrug his shoulders. One day he met her with a brighter smile. . . the high Lama who had recorded her birth experience was being returned to the temple to live out his final years. The original record had not yet been found. "But how will that help?" she said.

"Very simple, child," he teased her. "Don't you know that all lamas are trained in total recall? The High Lama is old but his mind is clear. He will meet with the others, recall the experience and they will verify it."

"Oh. And when will this happen?"

"In three days time. I spoke with the Lord Abbott about it this morning." He held her shoulders in his strong hands. "And so our friendship must end. It is not seemly for a chela to be consorting on rooftops with a priestess. I must go now. There is much ceremony to prepare for on the return of a High Lama."

She stayed until the wind and cold drove her to her room. Of course she was glad. Was this not the culmination of her entire life? Was she not privileged to be one of perhaps ten thousand women in the whole land to be even permitted to pass the portals of a temple. . . and to have the supreme accolade of priestess? Yes, she decided, she was happy. She was so happy she cried herself to sleep, wishing finally the old crone of her childhood was there to awaken her to do an hour of breathing exercises to harden the spirit within a frail body.

- 122 -

Told by Manoa-Ulmy that the consecration would take place immediately after the verification, Sutra-Scanore was awaiting him, dressed in the ceremonial robe her mother had grudgingly bought her for this occasion. She recognized his step before he turned the corner and ran several steps to meet him, but stopped when she saw his face, ashen-white and contorted with anger. She retreated from him, an arm raised to her face to avert the blow she knew must fall. His face softened but the urgency remained in his voice. "Go into your room and take off that robe and headdress. Dress yourself in the clothing in which you arrived, gather whatever possessions you have and come with me."

Numbed beyond comprehension, she obeyed, hearing the sound of his sandals as he paced back and forth before her door. Although she had come to hate the monotony represented by the tiny cubicle, she hesitated before leaving it for what she sensed was the last time. The questions began to form on her lips as she joined Manoa-Ulmy but he silenced her with a cruel grip on her arm as he hurried her through the now familiar corridors and out of the temple into the crystal clarity of the sunlight. Indignation overcoming her fear, she jerked her arm free. "What are you doing with me?"

"I am returning you to your parents. Come!"

Keeping step with him in preference to being dragged, she said, "But why?"

"I will explain when we are away from the temple. I do not wish to shed blood while wearing this robe," he said. And she knew fear again.

They walked for a half hour, then slowed and he led her into a small park. "It is not yet noon," he said. "We can rest here and I will tell you." They found a secluded spot to sit and she spread her ceremonial robe to cushion them from the cold earth.

"I hope you will tell me nothing more about the shedding of blood." Her voice shook.

"That was unfortunate," he said, sighing. "I was born under the sign of the twins and have a second nature of violence. I had hoped I had overcome it." He picked up a stone and traced a pattern on the ground with it. "That was another reason I was turned out of the lamasary." She knew by now he was speaking of the place where he had been in training. He referred to the place they had met as 'the temple' but the other in the more respectful term 'lamasary'. He made another effort to speak calmly, then blurted, "The damned old fool denies both your immersion and the birth recording!"

"The High Lama?" She gasped and moved to face him. She

had never heard a high lama spoken of except in terms of highest respect. "There must be some mistake. My mother's handmaiden took me to the temple herself. She told me."

"Of what value is that?" he said bitterly. "Who will believe the word of a serving girl against that of a High Lama?"

"It wouldn't make any difference," she said, catching his mood. "The girl told me she fell asleep and didn't witness the immersion. What did happen? Did the High Lama forget?"

"No, he didn't forget and I could tell from his aura that he was telling the truth."

"Well, what did he say? You were there."

"He only said, 'I did not see this female at her birth nor did I immerse her', and then he walked out. The other lamas turned on me and accused me of willfully harboring an imposter and to return you to your family forthwith. The accusations are what made me so angry."

"What will they do to you now?"

"They will do nothing because I will not return to the temple."

She let her hands fall into her lap and looked down. "And I cannot return to my family. Remember what they did to my brothers. Imagine what they will do to a mere female. A female imposter at that." She began to cry.

He shifted and took both her small hands in one of his. "Please don't do that. We must at least make the effort. I think there is a law governing these situations. Come. I will be with you."

They spoke little during the next two hours enroute to Sutra-Scanore's house. A servant had recognized her and her mother met them at the gate to the courtyard. Repelled by the woman's painted grossness and surprised at her age--he had expected her to be much younger--Manoa-Ulmy stated the reasons they were there in short, terse sentences. The woman heard him out, then threw her head back and shrieked, again and again. "Don't let her alarm you," Sutra-Scanore said tonelessly. "That's the way she calls my father."

A large man with rolls of fat jiggling around his middle hurried across the courtyard followed by two or three nervous servants.

Identifying the man as Sutra-Scanore's father, Manoa-Ulmy repeated his story. "Then why do you bring the slut to me?" the fat man said.

Manoa-Ulmy flushed dark but replied courteously. "She is your daughter, sire."

"None of your insolence, slave-monk!" the big man roared. "I'll have you know I've been well trained in wrestling. I'll break you in half if I must."

"I have been trained, too, Sire. You may find my training a bit more subtle." Manoa-Ulmy's eyes narrowed and concentration brought a furrow to his forehead. The fat man gasped and sank to the ground, moaning. With a slight bow to the now gaping mother, he took Sutra-Scanore's arm and walked away.

"What did you do to him?" she said when they were some distance from the house.

He squeezed her arm. "I gave him a headache."

"And now what are you going to do with me?"

"Take you home with me, of course."

"To your family? What will they say when they see me?"

"I assure you they will be more courteous than your family."

They laughed together, like children given an unexpected holiday, and spent a leisurely afternoon reaching his home, delaying until his father would be there.

Despite an acute pain of self-consciousness, Sutra-Scanore felt an immediate warming to the quiet dignity and mutual love she found in Manoa-Ulmy's family. He told the story before his mother would permit them to eat. They listened in silence, shaking their heads occasionally and exchanging sober looks. When the story was finished, the father stood, a sign that the others were to stand. "So you have brought me another daughter. She is welcome. We will eat now."

The meal was eaten in traditional silence. "With your permission, father, I have more to say," Manoa-Ulmy said. "I want to make Sutra-Scanore your daughter in truth and in fact."

The older man frowned. "There are certain precedures. . ."

"I am aware of that, father. As I explained to you before dinner, however, I have already had words with her family."

The father flashed white teeth in a quick smile. "You are a young man of many words, Ulmy," he said, using the familiar form of his son's name. "However, we must not falter in our duties of courtesy to those of higher station. I will send a messenger tomorrow. You will write the message in my name, as you know I am only accomplished in the accounting language of my business."

"They will only send him away," Sutra-Scanore burst out, then bowed her head in embarrassment at her temerity in speaking without being bidden in the presence of elders.

Manoa-Ulmy's mother moved to her. "So what is so terrible about a nameless messenger being sent from the doors of foolish people? My husband is right, child. We must observe the rules of our society, whether we relish them or not." She patted the girl's arm. "But we have heard many brave words from my son on this subject of marriage, and nothing from you. What is your feeling?"

Sutra-Scanore did not raise her eyes. "It is not a woman's place to speak of such things."

"That's nonsense, child," the woman said. "If you have no home, no social status and apparently not even an official name, you at least have a mind of your own. . . and you will be expected to use it with us."

"He did speak to me of such things this afternoon," she said shyly. "I am still fearful and confused but I would like very much to be his wife."

"Well spoken," the mother said. "It is good this virile looking son of mine has had no sympathy with this foolish celibacy cult I hear about."

"It does not matter, mother," Manoa-Ulmy said quietly. "I do not plan to return to the temple. I am sure my father can use two more strong and willing hands."

Manoa-Ulmy labored diligently but with little expertise for his patient father, counting the months until he could take Sutra-Scanore to his bed as his bride in fact if not in name. A half year of living with parents was considered an adequate waiting period but he would not consider the formal cermony until the stars of their respective signs were in the most favorable position. His hair had grown long and shaggy onto his neck when an excited messenger came to him one day in the market place and commanded him to attend an immediate Council of Lamas.

"Council of Lamas?" he said, uncomprehending. "Are you sure it is me you were sent to bring?" Yes, the acolyte explained, almost dancing in excitement. There was a great scandal brewing in the temple regarding the old High Lama. The old man was taken ill and was thought to be near death and had a matter of grave importance to reveal to the Council of Lamas.

Waiting only long enough to wash himself, Manoa-Ulmy went with the young acolyte to the temple where he was ushered direct-ly to the Council Chamber. From long training and habit, he bowed reverently to the gathering and seated himself on the floor. At that moment the old High Lama was carried through another door, sitting on a litter. Fluttering his palsied hands at the attendants to place his litter on the floor, the High Lama began to speak in a surprisingly strong voice. "I have no desire to endure the next segment of eternity wandering in the corridors of the damned. I have brought grief to the innocent and disgrace upon this temple."

He paused and drank steaming tea from a cup held by an attendant.
"I have caused others to stray from the true path by letting them
conceal my actions." He drew himself up and extended an arm to
Manoa-Ulmy. "This monk was to bring a novice priestess to me for
consecration and I had her sent away because neither the recording of the birth experience nor immersion had taken place.

"I spoke the truth. They did not take place because I was not
present to perform my annointed duties. I cannot excuse my actions nor rectify the damage I have caused but I hereby make a
dying appeal to this assemblage to make exception and proceed
with the consecration. As for myself, I have given instructions that I
be removed to the most remote temple which can be reached in
two days time and there I will live out my days in silence and
penitence."

Manoa-Ulmy wandered the streets of Lhasa after leaving the
temple. The Council of Lamas had remained in session after the old
High Lama had been taken away and within moments had approved Sutra-Scanore's readmission to the consecration ceremony. This rite was scheduled in abeyance until word would be received of the passing of the old High Lama. No possibility of residual
moral stain could be left to chance.

He returned late to his home, to a scene of subdued anxiety.
Contritely aware of his selfishness in brooding alone when the
family had known he was summoned to the temple, he told the
story as briefly as he could. Finally, in a choked voice he told Sutra-
Scanore to find and prepare her ceremonial robe and headdress.
He would return to the temple in the morning and again make the
necessary arrangements for her consecration.

She had listened without speaking during his recitation of the
day's events. Now, with a small smile on her face, she walked to
him, took his big hands and pressed them to her breasts. "What are
you talking about, you great fool?"

"I am talking of you and your duties. . . and of mine."

"Then you are talking nonsense." She moved near him. "My
first duty is to the man whose wife I have promised to be. Since the
temple women do not marry, how can I do both?"

Manoa-Ulmy looked to his parents, who shrugged and turned
to leave the room. With a glad cry swelling his throat, he lifted her
from the floor and overtook his father. "Father! After this night she
will be your daughter indeed. There will be no more waiting!"

It was long before Sutra-Scanore could accustom herself to the earthy informality of a working class family. Often when she would come to breakfast with her eyes still reliving the previous night of passion, her mother-in-law would smile and say, "Was it good, child?" Nor could the mother understand Ulmy's insistence on his wife taking a bitter substance to prevent conception until the stars were right. The older woman would listen patiently to her children's elaboration of astrological significances and then comment, "Your father and I turned the glory of the nights into children. When the gods willed it was time, the children stopped arriving but we still have our nights." She would chuckle contentedly and Sutra-Scanore would hunt for something to do in another room, blushing furiously.

When she professed an insincere interest in the wool business as an excuse to escape her mother-in-law's embarrassing conversations, the father took her to the market place. There he taught her the subtleties of bargaining and the art of figuring, talents which his son never mastered despite his bullish eagerness to be helpful. It was a fortuitious move, for many buyers came only to see and talk with a lovely young girl instead of a whining wool dealer's wife. These merchants parted with their money and goods at a premium but left with the self-righteous knowledge that they had not attempted to cheat such a charming and flashing-eyed creature.

It was the reputation of this business which, two years later, brought a messenger from the notorious Sheik of Wisontor. The Sheik had arrived two days before with, it was said, a caravan of a hundred shaggy camels laden with spices and dried fruits so dear to the drab Tibetan diet. It was rare when such an abundance of delicacies arrived in Lhasa but, despite their greed, the merchants and indeed the entire city was glad the Sheik visited only once every three or four years. There was dark talk of young girls and even young boys who had disappeared never to be seen again when the Sheik's caravan departed.

The messenger asked about the availability of large quantities of woven cloth of a specified quality. Sutra-Scanore assured him it would be there in two days time and the messenger left, saying the Sheik himself would come the following day to consummate the deal. Ulmy and his father had been talking in low voices in the background. Ulmy put an arm around Sutra-Scanore's shoulders. "I think it will be better if you are not here when the Sheik comes tomorrow."

She flashed him a smile. "Why not, you ninny? This will be the largest transaction we have made all year and I want to make sure the accounting is properly done."

"The Sheik's honesty in business matters is a matter of record," the father said. "His honor in dealing with women, however, is open to serious question. I also urge you to stay at home."

"You two are worse than a mother bird. What in the world could the Sheik do, tie me to one of his smelly camels and carry me screaming from the market place? I am sure even the great Sheik knows we are capable of encorcing the laws of our own land." Father and son argued at greater length but the smiling girl quieted them with her laughing ridicule.

Manoa-Ulmy and his father had a great quantity of the cloth assembled when the Sheik arrived, carried in a sedan chair by four beautifully muscled blacks who, stripped to the waist, seemed impervious to the biting chill. Ulmy and his father looked at each other, wondering at their misgivings about this shrewd but outgoing and jovial little man with such a dark reputation. The deal was completed within an hour and the Sheik, unused to dealing with women merchants, went to the back of the shop with the father to attend to details of payment and delivery. Parting with mutual affirmations of respect, the Sheik moved down the street in his magnificant chair. "There," Sutra-Scanore said, "is he really such a terrible man?"

The father stared at her with a strange look. "This jolly little man just made me a handsome offer for you. I declined but he said he would return with a final offer before he leaves the city."

She shivered. "I can't believe it. He seemed so. . . so civilized."

"You must remember, my daughter. . . such things are accepted in his civilization. Well, we have done a good day's work. Let us close early and go home."

Father and son conferred again before bedtime. "I am sure I saw one of the Sheik's men follow us home," Ulmy said. "What should we do? Many of the police monks are my friends. Perhaps I should send for them," he said, referring to the huge, seven-foot monks who kept order in the temples and were frequently pressed into service during crowded foast days in the city.

"I am also concerned," the father said. "But they have done no wrong. We will take her with us tomorrow so both of us will be near."

The next day was uneventful except for the dozen silent, powerful men from the Sheik who came and trotted away with the remainder of the cloth bales on their backs. They waitcd until late and no further word came from the Sheik or his men. They were further relieved when word came that the Sheik's caravan was loading in preparation for an early morning departure.

The women were in bed and father and son were having a final cup of tea when they were roused by a pounding on the barred gate leading to their small courtyard. The father went to the gate and, after identifying the man there as a trader whom he knew, admitted him. In the flickering light of the single lamp in the kitchen, Ulmy also recognized the man as a trader held in contempt by others as one who would perform any mission for a price. "What is it, man?" the father said. "It is time decent people were asleep."

"I come with a message from your betters," the man said, sneering. "The Sheik of Wisontor wants you to make your daughter ready to ride with him in the morning. There are bearers at the gate with gold and a horse laden with rare spices. The Sheik says he has spoken to you of this matter."

In one fluid motion, Ulmy grabbed the man, raised him over his head and calmly aimed him toward the door. "NO!" the father said. "I did not breed you to violence! And you," he said to the mother who was peering down the stairwell, "return to your room. This is no affair for women. Come, Ulmy, show the man out and we will tell his friends we have no interest in his offer."

The trader wriggled with terror as Ulmy held him paralyzed with one huge hand fastened to the nape of the man's neck. Choking, he offered no resistance as he was carried to the gate by his neck. Ulmy put him to the ground but did not release him. "Tell them," he said quietly.

With many gestures and phrases of a strange language, the trader spoke to three men who squatted beside a horse. One laughed and with incredible swiftness sprang to the father's back, a curved blade in his hand revealed in the silvery starlight. The father fell to the ground under the man's weight as Ulmy reached them. Ulmy ripped the man loose but the knife traced a deep pattern up his father's face and into his scalp. The father turned into the gateway, staggered a few steps and fell at his door. Ulmy took the man's knife hand and broke the wrist with the pressure of his own hand. Then with a powerful movement of his hand which he had learned well but had been cautioned never to use except in defense of his life, he crashed his fist against the side of the man's head, crushing it like an overripe fruit. The now faceless body fell beside his father as the mother came to the door. Seeing the two bodies and the blood, she turned and ran screaming back into the house.

Still moving with disarming deliberateness, Ulmy turned to the other two men, both with knives drawn but standing undecided outside the gate. "If you turn to statues in your tracks you may yet live to see another sunrise." The men did not understand the language but understood with awful clarity what had just happened to their companion. Ulmy picked up the body of the dead man and threw it like a bag of barley at the feet of the other two. He turned his head and heard the footsteps of the trader running up the street. "Trader!" he bawled. The footsteps slowed and stopped. "Come back, trader. I have a message for the Sheik. Come back, trader, or by the name of the Holy One himself I will find you before another day is born!"

Thus persuaded, the trader scurried back but maintained a respectful distance between himself and Ulmy. "Tell them to bind this body to the horse, trader, and deliver it to the Sheik. Tell the Sheik there is no law in any land to protect him from me if he attempts this form of crime again. Get out of my sight. You are bringing a fearful smell to the neighborhood."

Not waiting for them to leave, Ulmy strode to the house and bent over his father, then carried him tenderly into the house. The older man was unconscious and had lost much blood but was not, he could see, seriously hurt. He called his mother while rummaging for the herbs he would apply to the knife wound on his father's face. He called his mother again and was answered by an anguished shriek from upstairs. "Come, mother. It is over now. I need your help." He went to the foot of the stairs. "What's wrong? Come build up the fire for me. Father has been hurt."

He started up the stairs but his mother ran down, screaming, and almost overbalanced him. He held her weight while she clawed at his chest. "Dead!" she cried. "All dead!"

"No one is dead except the swine who hurt father. Try to control yourself. Father will be all right."

"No... .." she wailed. "Your wife. . . your Sutra is dead!"

"NO!" His voice was as the blast of an avalanche in the confines of the small house. He sat his mother on a step and ran up to his and Sutra-Scanore's room. There, gracefully curled in the center of the sleeping pad they had shared, she lay, quite dead. Reacting automatically to his years of training in the medical lamasary, he knelt and raised her face, then gently released it as he saw the burn marks left by the poison on her mouth. Her cheek was already cool when he stroked it a final time before joining his mother in the kitchen.

"Where are my boots, the ones she made for me?" he said.

The mother, her face slack with shock, stared at him. "Where are you going?"

"To kill the Sheik. Where are the boots?"

As in a nightmare, she rose and stood, barring his way to the door. "It was I who killed her. See to your father. There has been enough of death in this house."

He grabbed her shoulders. "What do you mean?"

"In my fear, I thought both you and your father were dead. I ran up to tell her. When we heard you return to the house, she thought it was the Sheik's men and swallowed the poison."

He held his mother while the great sadness grew in him. The poison. The little stone bottle always at hand, which she had sworn to take if he preceded her in the end of this lifetime. After all, she had repeated many times when he sought to take the poison from her, we are bound by forces stronger than this life. This was part of our training. Teasing, he had asked her if he should take the potion if she departed before him. She had an answer for this, too. He was the stronger and could survive without her. She could not survive without him. He held his mother from him and silently began reciting the prayer for the dead as he ministered to his father.

———————————————

Because Sutra-Scanore's spirit lived, and guided him, Manoa-Ulmy re-dedicated his own life to the service of the living. He returned and was readmitted to the lamasary for an additional ten gruelling years of training and prayerful learning. Well into life, he did celebrate a temple wedding, to another woman. He stood grave and thankful, attired now in the robe of a Medical Lama, and with a warmness in his heart he listened inwardly as he heard Sutra-Scanore's voice joined in the ageless, joyful chant for the union of spirits on earth.

———————————————

Once again we were not quite prepared for the sudden violence and death which ended another brief earthly mating. If that had been the end of the story we might have remained vaguely dissatisfied. Even so, we had to wait several years until others re-entered our present lives to fill in missing details.

After hashing over this chapter with us, Keetoowah also objected, claiming his long-time consort (he always refers to Carol as the Wild Witch, regardless of the setting of any lifetime of which we share recall) wouldn't have fallen apart and killed herself at the sight of a little blood. Perhaps not, but the stark fact that she always carried the vial of poison indicates a probable master plan she, as Sutra Scanore, was not aware of. Looking at the entire life in Tibet, it emerges that the significant mile post was the later elevation of Manoa-Ulmy to the important position of Medical Lama.

This has an interesting sidelight, brought to us by yet another person who has been in and out of my own time/space realms through more than one lifetime. We contacted a psychically sensitive lady at the behest of a friend. At our first meeting in the lady's home, she and I stared at each other then, laughing and crying, we embraced. This 'instant memory' included a childhood together as brother and sister, another as mates in India and her full knowledge of my life as Manoa-Ulmy in Tibet. She was also quick to grasp the eternal familial ties which hold us in such an affectionate bond with Keetoowah.

This contact dredged up another memory I approached with some delicacy. Repeated meditations followed by the now-familiar visualizations brought me back to one inescapable fact: Keetoowah had been with us yet again but not exactly as one of the good guys. Keetoowah was the ailing High Lama who had evaded his duties in recording the birth experience of Sutra-Scanore. I didn't want to embarrass him by bringing this up although it is an integral part of the story. My hesitancy wasn't justified. Prodded by my recall accounts, my old friend readily agreed he was the culprit and offered a broader view than I had been taking. It could have been no other way, he claimed, if events were to develop according to larger-scale planning.

The Tibetan lifetime was in a sense tailored for me. It had doubtless been decided I needed a life of discipline, austerity and service to curb a strong rebellious streak which had (and still has, Heaven help me) gotten me into hot water for eons. I don't remember any single incident which resulted in my early expulsion from the medical lamasary; I wryly suspect it was an accumulation of mild insubordinations which finally wore out the patience of my superiors.

In point of time, Sutra-Scanore had not been born when I first entered the medical lamasary as Manoa-Ulmy. I expect my behavior patterns were established early enough to make a fairly accurate pre- diction that I'd be booted out before completing my training. But I do not believe Sutra-Scanore elected this incarnation with the sole purpose of sacrificing herself to assure my return to the medical lamasary and even- tually achieve a place of stately prominence. I'm even tempted to accuse her of making one last effort to become a priestess after her many failures to thus make her mark in ancient Egypt.

However it was orchestrated, it is clear to me that Keetoowah directed this particular adventure. But would that mean he also took himself out of the picture at the most convenient time? Not quite. He, as a High Lama, was aged and tottering when he admitted his mistake and chose the penance for his actions. He directed that he be sealed into a cave with only a small opening for ventilation and for receiving a minimum food supply. "It's a good thing you didn't put something on the shelf temporarily while waiting for me to pass over in my cave," he remembered grimly. "I lived another thirty years." I believed him but shuddered at the thought of all those years spent in dank, total darkness. It is not surprising; the monks and priests of Tibet practiced a stern self-discipline rarely seen by today's world.

VII

A frequently heard description of outrageous behavior is, "Why, that isn't even human!" It would be interesting to know where and under what circumstances this phrase originated. I have had first-hand experience with cases of possession, wherein the body and mind of some inoffensive or careless person is invaded by an alien entity. I use the term 'alien' guardedly because for my immediate purposes I apply it to non-human life forms, entities with distinctive, individual personalities who are not, nor have ever been, 'human' in physical, emotional or intellectual make-up. Most instances of possession seem to be by earth spirits who formerly inhabited human bodies (usually angry) who are too ignorant to avail themselves of the more desirable reality where they are and want to repeat some earth experience, frequently of a socially unacceptable nature. On rare occasions, however, I have sensed the presence of non-human personalities. I make this statement in the pure realm of speculation and it is highly subjective, based on a skin-crawling alien quality I sensed from the things, coupled with a downright fear of the implacable, powerful evil of them. I have encountered them on several occasions but, thankfully, not often.

This is not to suggest that, because an entity appears as an alien within our own narrow human frame of reference, it is bad. A writer seldom has only one thing going for him at one time; there is almost invariably something else in the mill for, after all, this is where the next pay check is coming from. While researching past lifetimes, two areas presented themselves which were fascinating in their potential. Initially, we wondered what we did, thought and planned in the intervals between our earthly incarnations. This information is available but only by dredging our subconscious, and we have found this is a tedious process, requiring more physical and psychic energy than we have available at this time. To really expand, we hit on the idea of tapping ancient recall, memories extending backward to lifetimes shared before the formation of this particular solar system, and from this to begin laying the groundwork for a sequel to this writing.

Looking back, I suppose we advanced this proposal pretty brashly to our 'research team' but they didn't chide us for it. (And we were often chided, severely.) It is necessary to insert here, by way of introduction, the most potent guiding spirit we have on the next plane, that of my mother. My mother is a highly developed spirit and it is for this reason that I chose to be born of her flesh the last time I came to earth. She is so highly evolved that it was not until less than two years before beginning this book that I overcame the awe I felt in her presence and opened communication with her. I began by telling her I loved her and was sorry I hadn't been a better son. Those were the words which I hadn't said since her death, although I was frequently aware that she was there. At any given moment during the thirty-five years, I could have opened my heart and said, "Mother, I love you. Help me," and my life would have taken on the added richness it now has. Mother doesn't really belong where she is; she is trained for usefulness far beyond our comprehension. Yet she is staying with us for the remainder of this tenure of existence because we are into this thing up to our necks and we need her. She was also, at least once, Carol's mother so we are maintaining a close, albeit jumbled family relationship.

One day I received a 'call' from mother, answered it and was told to stand by for a very special communication. My mind was then taken over as it is when I go into a light trance, but the images which entered were beyond the human vocabulary. I had glimpses of mountains towering not in feet or meters, but MILES over a landscape which was predominately shaded in various tints of blue. I sensed rather than saw condensed forms of what appeared to be gaseous matter but which radiated love and life. I felt an intelligence attempting to blend with mine, bending, cooperating in every way trying to make me understand what it was. It didn't happen the way it was supposed to. I was conscious only of an unusual, consuming physical pain and a strange sense of disorientation. A complete communication was not established. Carol, who was with me, said my facial features were altered, and my voice. Carol was alarmed and took no notes; I was in enough of a trance to have little memory, so there is where the incident ended.

We were assured that, anytime I felt ready, the effort could be repeated, but with modifications. I have not felt ready yet, but the time may come. I was told that the experiment was an attempt to put me in contact with an alien entity with whom I had been acquainted eons ago when I, myself, had existed in that life form. The purpose was, hopefully, to release memories from a much deeper well which would be of value to me. Since there was no way I could communicate with this entity linguistically, it was permitted to enter my mind. I was told that, if we had succeeded, this would have been quite a breakthrough for us since very few earth minds have accomplished this. Some have, those with better trained and better disciplined minds, but I am not now a member of that select group. This is slightly bruising in the ego department but it is tempered with grateful love for those who are guiding us because they will wisely not saddle us with more than we can handle.

A young man came into our lives when I employed his wife to type this manuscript and act as our general part-time secretary. He is a United States citizen, she is a Mexican national. They had chosen to make their lives in Mexico for this time, as had we. Our initial, casual friendship developed as he learned more of the type of writing we now do. For purpose of identification, his name is Bill. Bill is the contemplative sort and it was not until we had known each other for some time that he asked us if it would be possible to probe his own past lifetimes. I assured him it was possible but not necessarily with us because this is an area in which we feel we have little in the way of qualified experience to offer to others. We had explored our own pasts, but only with prayerful, cautious guidance. We had copious material available for ourselves but we are a continuum; our cosmic vibrations, or whatever they are, remain attuned to some segment of our consciousness which has always existed, which is why we can actually remember so much of it. We were dubious about how accurate our receptivity would be when we attempted to attune it to a link in someone else's lifeline. I explained this.

He did some more cogitating and then revealed that he had spent four years of concentrated study of the I CHING, which I confess is largely beyond me, and that he spends part of each day in deep, serene meditation. We responded to this with warmth because we recognize true spirituality but we are excessively tedious in these things and now wanted to know WHY Bill wanted to learn of previous lives. Simple. Bill doesn't feel at home in his present body. He's awkward, uncoordinated, physically allergenic to almost everything and often possessed of what he calls a spiritual detachment. He wants to learn to cope with what he is, right here and right now. With this information and reassurance, we went to work.

Bill is an alien. This is the first time he has inhabited an anatomically physical body as accepted by our earth-life definitions. But he has had other lives on this planet, lives as an intelligent, functioning life-form. It was a form which tried to adapt to the geo-physical demands of this planet and failed, apparently repeating the attempt through a number of generations.

Bill is more fortunate than most because he knows the WHY of this particular lifetime. It is to coalesce all forms of 'human' expression into universal formulae. His work is his own and will be forthcoming but I bring him into this narrative perhaps only to reassure myself that aliens still stalk their measured miles over this planetary surface, and that their intentions are frequently honorable and productive, and good. Once, at least in our memory, Carol and I drew our sustenance from this earth while inhabiting 'alien' or not-quite-human bodies. We do not know how this came about nor just exactly what we were at that time but, as it must come to us all, we will learn. . . we shall eventually know. It is fortunate that I had much of this background before beginning the final lifetime we have chosen for this book.

I have followed the writings of certain science fiction writers because I respect their literary integrity. I love well-written fantasy but my reading interests have seldom been stimulated by science fiction. Purely a matter of personal taste. It required weeks to complete the narrative of this lifetime because every iota of my earthly conditioning resisted the inescapable fact that my mate and I shared not one but many lifetimes on this planet as a life form which cannot be accepted as human by contemporary definition. I persisted, our helpers persisted, but I still regard it as I would one of my own kids who had decided to isolate himself on a forgotten mountain in Pakistan, subsist on barley and rice and spend his remaining days contemplating his navel. I wrote it because other voices from other worlds urged me to, but I did it under protest. When it was completed, I was glad. It closed a gap of understanding we would not have gained otherwise. I wrote it as I received it.

The tall man who had borne the name of Xanthu for nearly ten thousand years strode the broad walkway which formed the top of the temple walls. Wisps of steam still rose around him as the blast of the sun vaporized the moisture from the brief but torrential rain of half an hour before. Xanthu stopped in a characteristic pose of utter motionlessness and stared at a hillside a few miles distant. Through dint of relentless work the hillside had just been cleared of jungle and the workers rewarded with a seven-day rest-time. As Xanthu stared, the hillside appeared to become noticably greener, as if the soul of the jungle stirred beneath the soil, flexing itself to again burst forth and consume the results of many months labor.

Xanthu knew how to conquer the jungle. Machines could be built which would alter the molecular structure of the growth, reducing it to rich, thick, fertile loam to nurture the crops for future generations. But such machines required technical knowledge, knowledge that even with hypno-learning would take another three centuries to develop. Mining and the refining of metals had only begun during the present century; this had made possible cutting instruments which had kept the jungle at a standoff but it required almost all available labor for this. There was so precious little time left for teaching, for leading the race into the heritage that was theirs.

Too little time left over after basic survival to reverse the mind control that had reduced this new human race to willing, placid laborers for the Rulers.

Xanthu had been born in this place but, with access to everyone else's memory, he let his mind rest briefly on the history of this new land. He and his mate had not been in body when his race had scorched the old home continent while tampering with the regional magnetic field. The resulting atmospheric friction neutralized all power-driven machinery, including air and surface transportation. Struggling to survive this chaos, the nation's scientists did not realize for several years that the disturbed atmosphere was becoming increasingly hotter.

Many escaped before the land mass broke up and finally sank. Air and land temperatures rose at a steady rate but the increase was so gradual that time remained to build sail and muscle-powered ships. Most fled to large islands and sparsely populated subcontinents halfway around the world. Others chose the frontier of the great land mass over the western horizon, a threatening area of towering mountains, jungles and angry rivers. The continent was called Aya and, although it had been explored and mapped, was regarded as too geologically unstable for settlement.

A pioneering group of the Rulers gathered as many of the docile workers as they could logistically support and began a migration to the new land. Several thousand Rulers and workers reached the forbidding shores, bringing basic survival equipment, portable machines and a few crystal powered energy accumulators. This enabled them to penetrate the jungle to a fairly hospitable area, clear the land for cultivation and lay out and build a magnificently functional city. Then the machines failed. Scrupulously serviced and maintained, many machines lasted a century. But without a central power source to renew their molecular structure they ground to a halt and were dismantled and the metals used to fashion more primitive hand tools. In time these, too, deteriorated and were forgotten soon after they were discarded. The Rulers salvaged some laboratory equipment constructed of a virtually indestructible material it was no longer possible to reproduce. Carrying a monstrous guilt for ages of exploitation of the planet's natives, the Rulers toiled endlessly to rebuild a civilization but every generation saw a steady decline.

There was only time to keep the small brown people healthy, encourage them to procreate, try to overcome the baffling problem of shortened lifetimes which made them old at sixty and usually dead ten years later. And there was the never-ending vigil to keep the young, developing Rulers who had not yet attained to the Memory from mingling and mating with the working Ayas. All knew the penalty; it was taught from birth and read in public proclamation twice each year, yet every temple technician had lost at least one student through this infraction. . . and with each loss the Rulers became weaker, less able to ensure the continuation of this civilization they had vowed to protect and save. With this thought, Xanthu felt a pain tingle at his consciousness, knowing the decision he would have to render to his mate Tsunor. His mind told him Tsunor would meet him in this place within the hour.

Aware of her presence in the closed courtyard below, he turned to watch her cross it to the inner stairs which would lead her to him. His mind filled with the old pleasure he always felt when he was near her and he turned his mind casually back over the many lifetimes they had shared together, again thankful that they had met again in this one. The greatest number of survivors of their kind, he knew, lived on another continent halfway around the world but of their successes in rebuilding a civilization he knew little.

Tsunor entered the temple below and in a few moments stood beside him. He took her hands and drew her to him briefly. "You come early," he said.

"There was no cause for delay," she said, speaking aloud because she knew he liked the sound of her voice. "You already know the results of the tests."

"Yes," he said, turning away from her. "The girl is three months pregnant. . . and by one of the temple workers."

"And for that she must die," Tsunor said. It was a tentative question, prompted by her memory of the stricken resignation on the young girl's face when she was brought in for examination a few days before.

"She must die," Xanthu said after a long pause. He turned to her again and sought to ease her sadness with words which they both knew but repeated to each other at these times. "We know she cannot carry the child because such children are born uninhabited and rarely live more than a few days. If we could only overcome this genetic mis-match we could hopefully at least breed our longevity into them."

"I know," she said, "But you have been training this girl yourself since birth. It seems such a waste."

"It's a terrible waste," he said. "But you saw the results of the tests before I did. The infusion of the foreign genes into the girl's body have already caused an irrevocable emotional warp. She would not develop beyond where she now is and she's potentially dangerous."

"Was she a good student, Xanthu?" Tsunor said, still unwilling to accept.

"She was marginal," Xanthu said. "There was serious question as to whether she would survive the Transition. You may read the report." He closed his eyes and opened his mind to her so she could scan the meticulous mental notations he had available at all times through total recall.

Tsunor squinted in concentration for a few seconds, then sighed. "It seems we are always losing them, in one way or another. It is such a shame they must always die. You could downgrade her mind, Xanthu, and sterilize her. Then she could live happily with her worker-mate."

"What kind of happiness would it be to have no will, to feel no emotion?" he said, his own anguish making his voice sharp. "And there will be no more altering of minds, my dear. I only ask you to remember how we, the two of us, misused mind control, stunting many generations before ancient Muror crumbled into the sea."

"Those are not proud memories, Xanthu," she said, looking down.

"Nor for me," he said. "Which is why we must be strict with ourselves. There are fewer than a thousand of us remaining, a decrease of nearly half in little over a hundred years since we were born to this life."

"Yes, and most of the females of child-bearing age are barren, as I am," she said. "Even the worker population has stabilized at less than sixty thousand."

"The jungle is winning," he said, glaring at the dark green which stretched to the limit of his eyesight. "I wish those who made the escape and colonized this damnable land could have forseen how the last polar shift would affect the vegetation."

She smiled, to lighten his mood. "We were between lifetimes then. I'm sure you wouldn't have let it happen had you been here in body."

"Of course not. I would have moved the beastly globe back to its original position with my bare hands." He returned her smile and held her to him again. "There is still hope. . . and still our obligations. Forgive me. I'm gloomy and bad tempered when we have a failure."

"We have become almost human this time," she said. She pulled back to look in his face. "Has it been decided how the girl will die?"

"I have suggested the gradual method," he said. "I think it will be accepted. I will stay with her and project her mind to the other side, a little longer each night. By the time when we must destroy her body she will be more at home there than here."

"That will be very tiring for you," she said.

"It will be well worth it if we can avoid any possibility of a trauma during the cross-over, and fortunately the girl's mind is adept enough for that."

"You are right," Tsunor said. "Do you recall the time we were drowned at sea, as children, before we were trained in the Memory? We must have been in a state of shock for over fifty years over there."

"Almost a century by current reckoning," he said. And as they shared this memory, they opened their minds and consciousnesses to each other, and to many memories. They had been born in the temple, within a few months of each other, almost a hundred and twenty years before. Their parents still lived but during this, the final phase of the Rulers' existence, the family unit style of living had been abandoned for the more utilitarian communal life. They remembered, although they had not understood at the time, the excitement in the temple when it was determined that they were mates, joined again to continue life which had already been shared through the sweep of countless eons of time and space.

Because they comprised such a potent force as a team, their mind training was accelerated and completed within fifteen years. The final opening of their consciousness to complete memory was the cause for great elation when it was determined that Xanthu was a proficient mind control technician and his mate Tsunor had complemented his work for many lifetimes as a body healer. However, they shared only with each other the memory of their discussions of suicide when the Memory revealed how they had manipulated the race indigenous to the planet for their convenience and, sometimes, amusement. . . altering genetic growth to produce powerful dwarfs to work the mines, reducing potentially intelligent beings to happy morons, in-breeding grotesque life forms to exhibit at professional fairs. The almost killing shock was the realization that they had done this not once but in many successive lifetimes. They asked for an additional three months rest-time after the temple Memory-clearing, which was granted in deference to their youth and status as soul-mates. They wandered in solitude through the lovely symmetry of the city which had taken three centuries to build, a city still largely unpopulated because the up-breeding of the race had taken far longer than anticipated.

The two, Xanthu and Tsunor, sealed themselved into their cubicles at the temple and took their spirits back to before birth, to the thousand years of silent penitence they had subjected themselves to in their own world while the earth had heaved and cracked and a continent slid piecemeal into the mud of the ocean floors. And through this experience they came again to life on earth, a life they had planned together, a life dedicated to the service of a people they had used so casually for so long. But their waiting extended over additional centuries until they could re-enter the world together, as male and female, as mates. They knew, perhaps more poignantly than the other Rulers, that their efforts would be painstakingly ineffectual but their dedication was such that, once begun, they would not deviate from their purpose. With the added power of combined consciousness, they also knew that theirs would probably be the last generation of Rulers so the responsibility rested heavily on them.

They had worked as a perfect unit for over a hundred years, he preparing the minds of the young born to the Rulers for the Memory-opening while she, the healer, sought to strengthen and fortify the bodies against the sometimes fatal trauma of suddenly recalling tens of thousands of lifetimes spanning perhaps millions of years. The loss rate was appallingly high. Many, when the concept of eternity came rushing to their present consciousness, could not absorb it and quietly returned to the world of greater reality from whence they had come. Xanthu and Tsunor berated the lack of proper equipment, watched the unexplainable decrease in births among their own kind and lamented the loss of two-thirds of the young who reached Memory-opening age. At the earth age of one hundred and twenty, they formed the active, hard-working nucleus of the "young ones". The majority of the population was older, still functioning in perfect bodies immune to disease and aging, but they had become mind-weary and discouraged. Every year more of them petitioned for permission to make the Return Transition, to leave their bodies and the earth.

A sound from the courtyard below brought them back to the present. Two of the Rulers had been escorting a worker across the area when the small man stopped and began to complain in a loud voice. The Rulers, with infinite patience and courtesy, let him speak, his voice rising to a shout while he made gestures to the skies with his arms. "It is the girl's lover," Tsunor said. "They are taking him from the temple to work in the fields."

"I know," Xanthu said. He stepped to the edge of the parapet and called down. "Stay, there. Bring him up here."

In a few moments the man stood between them and the two Rulers who had brought him disappeared silently back down the stairs. "Why do you complain?" Xanthu said pleasantly. "Do you feel we are being unjust to you?"

The man threw his head back and howled. "You're going to kill her! Why don't you kill me instead?"

"But you have done no wrong," Xanthu said gently. "The ruling applies only to us."

Tsunor put a hand on Xanthu's arm. "Wait." To the man, "Do you really love the girl so much?"

The man stopped in mid-howl, a puzzled expression on his face. "One does not presume to love a goddess," he said in a shocked voice.

"But you lay with her," Tsunor said. "A man like yourself, who has been educated and trained in the temple, does not take a woman like an animal, just because she is female."

"She is very beautiful and very desirable," the man said. "But she told me she could not bear children. She said all female Rulers are now barren."

Tsunor sighed. "Unfortunately, most of us are. But not all. We are a different race and because we are different, we are a dying race in your civilization. Because of what this girl has done, we will die a bit sooner."

"Everyone knows this," the man said, tears now running down his face. "But we can't understand why you waste yourselves like this. I know the baby couldn't live, but couldn't you take it from her and let HER live?"

Tsunor spread her hands helplessly, her own eyes dark with emotion. Xanthu frowned slightly in concentration, probing the man's mind. The man rubbed his forehead with the heel of his hand and said, "I know what you're doing, sir, but I wish you wouldn't. It's uncomfortable."

"I mean you no harm," Xanthu said. "I am only checking the depth of your understanding. You have been in the temple since birth, correct?"

"Yes. My parents were temple workers."

"I know," Xanthu said. "I remember when your parents were born. Back to the matter at hand. You have asked a reasonable question and you deserve a reasonable answer. I am sorry, but you would not be able to comprehend the answer we would have to give to your question."

"You always say that," the man said miserably.

Xanthu smiled. "Not always. Now it is you who are being unfair. You have learned much with us, you have advanced much further than your parents. I know you. Your name is Albar."

Surprised, the man looked up into Xanthu's face. "But you always act so, so. . ."

"Aloof?" Xanthu said. "Yes, we keep ourselves apart. One reason is that we are very busy but principally we want you to learn to live independently of us. As my mate just mentioned, we are finished as a race, perhaps with this generation."

"But you live forever!" the man said indignantly.

Tsunor knelt gracefully so the man would not have to look up to her. "Everyone lives forever, Albar. We just exist in different forms." She raised her hand to stop his interruption. "Yes, we do live longer. We can live for centuries on this earth whereas you cannot expect to reach a hundred. We have tried to remedy this but have failed."

"And now I'm being turned out of the temple," Albar cried.

"Not as punishment," Xanthu said. "It is better that you not be near as the girl makes her Return Transition. You may return to your duties later this year."

"After you've killed her," Albar said bitterly.

Xanthu's face became impassive. His mind raced through probabilities, objections, procedures. Tsunor, turned to his thoughts, at first recoiled from them, questioned them and finally acquiesced. Together they sent their thoughts to the Council, asking permission. When the affirmative answer came they glanced at each other and sat on the parapet, inviting Albar to sit between them. "I am going to make you an unusual offer, Albar," Xanthu said. "If you choose, you may remain with us, and the girl, during her Return Transition."

Albar looked at his feet, kicking a pebble across the walkway with a raspy, bouncing sound. "I know what you're telling me and I appreciate it. You want me to be here so I will know for myself that you won't hurt her. I already know that but, just the same, I'd have to watch her die. I don't want to do that. I watched my parents die and that was enough. But thank you for the offer."

"There is more than that," Xanthu said. "We are offering you an opportunity to see what none of your race has yet seen, other planes of existence, of life, which coexist with this one. I have already determined that your mind is flexible enough to understand much of it. Do you want to do it?"

"With all due respect," Albar said with the civility trained into him from birth, "why should I? What purpose could it accomplish?"

"It could give you knowledge to pass on to others of your kind," Xanthu said. "Most important, it will reveal to you that we are not really gods but just another life form. It is important that your race survive because we know that ours cannot. To survive you must accept spirituality into your consciousness. You must become aware of the higher power which governs the universe."

"But YOU are the higher powers. We worship you," Albar said.

"You are in error, but we are at fault. Soon, by our reckoning, we will be gone. Your descendents will forget us because, being telepathic, we will leave no written records. As you develop you will worship the sun, the moon, the earth itself because we will attempt to leave in you at least a subliminal awareness of spirit."

"But what does all this have to do with the girl?"

"I will guide her spirit, which does not die, into the cosmos from which it came. I will let you accompany her. It may take many weeks, or even months to accustom her memory again to the life she temporarily departed to come to earth."

There was silence while Xanthu and Tsunor tactfully refrained from intruding on the man's mind. A breeze fluttered Tsunor's robe against the parapet with a slight rustle. A burst of group song from some distant celebration came faintly to them. Albar took a deep breath. "I do not know what you are saying, Xanthu. Such things have never come into my mind. But I know you have never harmed us. We worship you. . ." He corrected himself. "We love you, so I will do as you ask."

Xanthu smiled and felt warmth at the man's intelligence. "Good. We will begin tonight. With your permission, I will put you into a deep sleep so you will be refreshed. Go to your room and to bed. I will come for you when the city sleeps."

———> <———

At the end of fourteen days Xanthu came again to his mate in the early hours of the morning. They met in the suite of rooms which had been assigned to them when they were mated in the temple. The two large rooms were in the living annex of the temple, connected by a half mile of thatch-covered passageway. As their rank was established they had been offered roomier, more sumptuous quarters but had declined because their rooms, on the second floor of the two-story building, gave direct access to the roof via a ladder in the corner of their bedroom. Since sleep was a luxury rather than a necessity, they spent many nights on their rooftop with hands joined, in silent communion with each other and the universe around them which they could now only touch with their minds and memories. "You have shut yourself from me during these days," Tsunor said softly. "It is difficult to continue as only a half-soul."

Xanthu accepted the words as they were intended, not as chiding but as a reaffirmation of their eternal closeness and belonging to each other. "There are difficulties I had not anticipated," he said. "Did you tune yourself to my report to the Council?"

"No," she said. "I was busy in the clinic and neglected to request permission. I knew you would be here soon for a rest-time. What has happened?"

Xanthu stripped and stood in the alcove letting the accumulated rain water from the reservoir on the roof run over his body. When he had finished she dried him with a soft cloth and led him to their pallet which was raised to let them lie against the wall by the single large window. She lay him on his stomach and soothed him by generating and passing small static electrical charges from her fingers into his muscles. "The girl is resisting the Transition," he said.

"How and why is she doing that?" Tsunor said, her surprise causing her to stop her manipulations and sit back from him on her knees.

Exasperated, he twisted himself to a sitting position and faced her. "How in the name of the blazing sun am I supposed to know that?" Seeing that his anger had not reached nor hurt her, he continued. "I have grasped the girl's mind, which is more pliable, more flexible than I had thought. She joined me almost immediately in the spirit and dropped her earth-tied emotions as easily as my body shed this water. But in a very sweet and reasonable manner. . . she just refuses to go."

"And what of the man. . . Albar?"

Xanthu lay on his stomach again to let her resume her massage. "He goes into spirit easily enough. I have not been able to devote sufficient energy to him to enable him to separate his spirit experiences from what he calls his dreams. He has learned the basics of telepathic communication from the girl so we have at least a positive gain to balance my negative results."

"Have you participated in any of their discourses?"

"No," he said. "I have not been invited."

She nodded, understanding the inviolable rule of their kind which dictated absolute respect of privacy. Concepts such as depths of comprehension, mental and emotional stability. . . such things as dealt with the health of the individual. . . could be investigated but intrusion into personal thoughts or conversations was unthinkable. "Has she given any reasons or explanations other than her natural ties to the earth?"

Xanthu stood with his hands on his hips and stretched. "Ah, that feels good," he said. "Thank you." He wrapped himself in a robe against the pre-dawn chill brought by the tropical rain "She says only that she will tell me when I have ceased my efforts to aid her in the Return Transition. Her attitude makes ME feel like the pupil."

"Has she given you any indication as to what she's talking about?"

"Yes, she says she has an important mission to perform on earth. She has even taken a name for herself. . . she calls herself Quetzie."

"Ketsie. . .?"

"Quetzie," he corrected her. "She speaks strangely of being the foreshadowing of a coming leader of the workers."

Tsunor became excited. "Do you think she is endowed with precognition, perhaps a genetic throwback to what we lost thousands of years ago?"

He smiled at her and she could see the fatigue of two strenuous weeks in his eyes. "I will surmise nothing until she has opened her mind to me. And she will not do that until I halt my efforts to carry her over. And I cannot even approach the Council for permission to stop until I have more substantial evidence. It is an impasse."

"What are you going to do?" she said.

"I will leave her to her own devices and turn to Albar. I want to spend more time leading him to conscious awareness of the spirit." He stretched himself again. "But right now I am going to love you fiercely and passionately for four hours and reward myself with a twenty-hour sleep period."

Her eyes shone as she stepped to him. "Let us try one hour of the madness and passion and then you will sleep twenty-three hours."

Xanthu came into the clinic and sniffed suspiciously over Albar's shoulder as the smaller man poured gritty black granules into a steaming ceramic pot on a charcoal brazier. "Please don't tower over me, Xanthu," Albar said without turning. "Sit. It will be finished momentarily."

Xanthu kicked a small pad into a corner and sat on the floor. "I stand, I do not tower," he said.

"When a seven-and-a-half foot man stands over a five-and-a-half foot man, he towers," Albar said, taking the aromatic smelling brew off the fire.

They shared a minute or two of silence while Albar peered into the pot to watch the clear hot water turn to a rich inky blackness. He poured it into two clay mugs and saluted Xanthu with a mocking, smiling toast. "To your ill health, my friend."

Xanthu scowled and sipped at his mug. "This wretched drink of yours contains a stimulant plus almost indigestible acids." He smiled, his face taking on a quick radiance. "And it tastes good. I deplore the future of your race when you learn to convert fruit to intoxicants."

Albar laughed and wrapped his hands around the mug. "We already have. All that remains is to find the proper agent to arrest the fermentation at pecisely the right time. Do you know what it is?"

"No," Xanthu said gloomily. "Our biologists would know but I'm sure they would not tell you. We used it in past ages as an anodyne for the workers when they became too old to be productive."

Albar smiled. "So even in those days you did not kill us when we were not useful? Did you kill each other, as you do now?"

"We separated the souls from the bodies when they became in-efficient or when genetic imperfections manifested themselves. . . or when we became tired and desired to depart for a rest and return in a renewed form. Oh, Albar, you must grasp the indestructability of the soul. We differ from you but only in form. We all are a part of the same life force and we all will live forever."

Albar settled himself comfortably on the pad beside his mentor. "Now you are the one who is being difficult. Do you think we could have this kind of conversation if I didn't believe you were a hundred thousand years old?"

"A conservative estimate," Xanthu said, reaching for the pot to refill his mug.

"Some part of me is aware of that, too," Albar said, "but I'm afraid my mind has gone as far as it can go. I simply cannot comprehend eternity."

"There is yet time," Xanthu said. "We have only worked together for three months and you're already an adept telepath and astral traveler."

"There is not time, Xanthu! Quetzie is beginning to swell with the child I put in her. Isn't the pregnancy term the same for you as it is for us?"

"A few weeks longer, I believe. There has not been a full term during my lifetime. Is there anything you can tell me about her? At your request, I have seen little of her during the time we have worked together. The Council is becoming impatient and I have no answer for them. And you must concede, my friend, there is no justice or even purpose in bringing a child into the world with no spirit to sustain its body."

"We have talked much of that," Albar said, pouring the last of the contents of the pot into his cup. "We do not want you in trouble with the Council. We do have something to tell you which may interest the Council. May I call her?"

Xanthu nodded, then jerked his head up in surprise. Albar's mind was open, inviting Xanthu to share for the first time in their communication. The answer came instantly and Xanthu felt the amusement in the girl's thoughts, a lilting pixie-laugh of high good humor. Should she, she asked, wear her ceremonial headdress for the great Teacher and Ruler or would it be acceptable if she rinsed her bulging, grotesque body in clean water and appeared to them in the proper garb of an obedient pupil. They all laughed and Xanthu said if she was really that unsightly, vanity was hardly appropriate. She flounced a reply to them and Albar suggested they move from the antiseptic atmosphere of the clinic to a small balcony sheltered from the sun.

The girl appeared a quarter of an hour later, her hair damp and hanging in a glistening black mantle over her shoulders. In her robe her pregnancy was not apparent but she pulled it close to call their attention to it. "I cannot do the proper obiesence without toppling over. . . and a toppled seven-foot woman cannot be grace-ful." She knelt on the pad and kissed Xanthu affectionately on the lips.

He returned her embrace and pulled her to sit beside him. "I have missed you, Quetzie. How have you filled your time?"

"I have not been idle. I have been infiltrating the brains of the Old Ones." She turned to Albar. "Is there tea?"

"The water is heating," Albar said, rising to re-enter the clinic.

"Whatever you're doing is probably good for them," Xanthu said. "Some of them have done nothing but sulk since the Council denied them permission to depart last year. I can sympathize with them but am glad for the delay since it would fall to me and my clinic to separate them from their bodies." He drew in his legs as Albar returned with the steaming tea and three mugs. "Although we will meet again it isn't an easy thing to bid farewell to a friend of a hundred years, even temporarily."

"Why do you keep them?" Quetzie said. "One must become awfully tired after three hundred years of life spent in an area of a few square miles."

"We need them most for their accumulated knowledge of this part of the earth. The most perfect communication is no match for actual experience. And we need them as teachers for our child-ren."

"Where ARE the children. . . OUR children?" Quetzie said.

Xanthu looked at her, puzzled. "What are you talking about?"

She laughed and held his hand. "Oh, Xanthu, you are the dearest person in the universe but you have no eyes in your head. Where are the Rulers' children? I am twenty years old or thereabouts and I am the youngest person in the temple. There are no children and there will be none. Haven't you and that stodgy old Council accepted that fact yet?"

"But so many of us are sterile. . ."

"All the men are and most of the women. . . but not all. I may be mistaken but I don't believe your generation has produced even one child. My own parents were over two hundred when I was born, as were the parents of all my generation."

Xanthu took a deep breath. "You are substantially correct, Quetzie. We have produced a few offspring among the fertile women of our age group but only through insemination. That is unsatisfactory because we reject the idea of producing children simply for the sake of breeding. Nor can we match fertile couples at random because most are mated and it would be in violation of our code of conduct."

"Your precious code has doomed you as far as earth life is concerned," Quetzie said primly.

He pulled her head to his shoulder and ruffled her hair. "And I suppose you have a solution."

"We have an idea," she said. "To us it sounds possible. To me it is preferable to living an interminable three or four hundred years while watching the jungle devour our people."

"Do you want to tell me about it?"

She gave him a quick smile. "I will let Albar tell you. You still treat me and think of me as a small child."

Self-conscious at using his newly-learned telepathic abilities with his teacher, Albar was silent for the time it took to finish his tea, assembling his thoughts. The actual transmission required less than a minute but the proposals were so radical, so foreign to everything the free-thinking Xanthu had practiced during his present earth tenure, that the tall Ruler was silent in return, only nodding when Albar offered to refill his mug. Excusing himself, he turned to his own mind, reviewing the intricacies of spirit transference and survival he had learned and practiced for thousands of years. At last he spoke. "Even if successful, it would be a mutation." But his voice was neutral, not encouraging but neither was it a denial.

Sensing an advantage, Albar continued verbally. "Mutation is the natural law of development on this planet, Xanthu. Your own memory must tell you of the changes in life forms, in vegetation, animals. . . every change began with a mutation somewhere."

"With your powers of persuasion, I should step aside and let you present these thoughts to the Council yourself," Xanthu said.

"Does that mean you have accepted them?" Quetzie broke in quickly.

"By no means," he said gently. "There is much I do not know, questions for which I have no answers. Remember I function effectively only as my mate functions. I cannot interrupt her now. Will you come to eat with us this evening at the hour of sundown?"

The meal was finished when Tsunor rose to light the lamps and place them on low stands around the room where their light caused huge shadows to chase each other across the walls and ceiling. The cured sap from a waxy jungle tree gave a clear, smokeless flame and filled the air with a faint but pleasant pungence. "You seem to enjoy our vegetarian diet, Albar," she said.

"That is Quetzie's doing," he said. "She has done all the cooking since I moved into her rooms." He relaxed and looked at his friends, the ones who so recently he had regarded as gods, and marveled again at their calm acceptance of his cohabitation with Quetzie, a taboo he had believed was so stringent that it was never spoken of even among his friends although it was common knowledge that many of them had lain with the young female Rulers.

"This diet contributes much to our longevity," Tsunor said.

"With what I have learned of your responsibilities, I am not sure I would desire to live long," Albar said, and added quickly, "Although I do plan to stay with this type of food."

"Your body will thank you," Tsunor said. "Shall we talk now? I know of your wishes from Xanthu but an open discussion will make things clearer for us all. Quetzie, since I'm sure this originated with you, we will let you begin."

Quetzie bit her lip in thought. "We cannot separate this from emotion, so I will begin by saying that as a woman with a body capable of bearing children, I want to use it for that purpose."

"I can understand that," Tsunor said softly.

"I meant no offense," the girl blurted.

"None taken. Please continue."

"I have spent much time with the Old Ones. They are unhappy because they do not feel they are contributing anything. . . and they are resentful because they are not permitted to leave their bodies."

"We know about that," Xanthu said. "We regret it very much."

"I wasn't really serious when I first mentioned it to them," Quetzie said. "I just said something like, wouldn't it be nice if one of the Old Ones could inhabit the baby I'm carrying in my body now. It was like a flash of lightning. They were all excited and insisted we ask you about it."

Tsunor gazed at the girl, a slight smile on her face. "Quetzie, you are not asking permission. . . you want to know if it is possible. Let's look at the facts. First, you know we cannot separate your spirit from your body. . . take your life, as Albar would say. . . without your permission. Likewise, we cannot take the baby from your body without your consent. These conditions are bred so strongly into our consciousness that we could not violate them even if it were determined it would be the wiser course."

"Are you suggesting that I'm taking advantage of you because I know these things?"

Tsunor laughed, a musical, rising sound. "Of course you are. If you wish, we will discuss the reasons later. If not, they will remain your secret." She became serious. "However, the questions surrounding the possibility of doing this thing are formidable."

"I imagine the most difficult would be in getting the permission of the Council," Albar said.

"No," Tsunor said. "Council permission is a mere formality. . . if the probabilities of success are at least equal to those of failure."

"But think of the incredible possibilities if we succeed!" Quetzie cried. "I will be of child-bearing age for at lease a hundred and fifty years which means I could have up to a hundred children. It has been done. . . we were taught that. If there were only ten women who are as fertile as I am we could have the beginnings of an entire new race within two centuries. . . stronger, more intelligent. We could defeat the jungle by sheer numbers!" Quetzie leaped to her feet, her arms outstretched.

Tsunor rose and put her arm around the girl's waist. "Child, child. This excitement is bad for your blood pressure in your condition. For your information, there are more than ten women of your generation who have child-bearing potential. About a hundred, I think. You would have a new race, yes, but a more primitive race than this one because you would not have access to the Memory. The skills learned by this current race would be remembered and refined but the great advances . . the use of atomic power, even electricity, the elimination of disease, the building of ships that will go either on the water or in the air. . . all this could take thousands of years without the Memory to guide you."

Quetzie was silent as she was led on a circuit of the room and back to sit with the men. "It would offer a better chance for racial survival than what we are doing now," she said quietly. "Of what value is the Memory after we as a race are no longer here to administer it?"

"Your point is well made," Tsunor said. "It will be given full consideration with all other aspects. Now you should know some of the problems which would be faced in such an undertaking. To begin with, you will not have an unlimited supply of spirit donors. We now total fewer than a thousand. Some, perhaps many, will not be willing to inhabit a new earthly body. I can tell you now that Xanthu and I will not. And there is no way to determine that YOUR offspring will be able to breed. Next, we would have to undertake extensive and purely experimental work to assure at least minimal compatability of the spirit donor to the child you will bear. There may have to be genetic alteration. . . the child will be born with many of the physical characteristics and personality traits of Albar, it's father."

"I have thought of all that," Quetzie said.

"But have you thought further? This probing, this compensation, this alteration would have to be done on your physical body, possibly even requiring surgery. You would be taking the risk of a painful physical death such as our race has seldom experienced on this earth. Even worse is the very real possibility of insanity which could plunge you into a dark and long-lasting trauma when you are forced to return to the existence from whence you came."

"Truthfully, I had not thought of these dangers," the girl said, her face tense. "My decision is the same. If there are even remote chances of success, I want you to make the attempt."

Xanthu leaned on an elbow and turned to face her. "Your determination has to do with your reasons for the entire undertaking, doesn't it?"

"Yes," she said, "and I choose not to discuss it at this time."

"And what of Albar?" Xanthu said. "He will have grown old while you are still young."

Albar chuckled, a contented sound deep in his throat. "It is time for me to point a way in which WE are different, Xanthu. We evolved as natives of this planet; you developed on another, in another star system. Racially, we are much younger than you. Younger, more carefree and perhaps more irresponsible. On this planet you mate for life or, as with you and Tsunor, for eternity. We mate when the blood runs hot. Sometimes the blood cools and each finds another mate. I love Quetzie, but I love you and Tsunor in much the same way. I could never regard Quetzie as my mate nor could I feel possessive or jealous."

Tsunor rose to her knees and spread her arms. Responding to this instinctive gesture, the others assumed the same position and they embraced each other. "You will have a baby, Quetzie," Tsunor said. "That is the only assurance I can give you at this moment. Xanthu and I will seal ourselves in here for a few days, or as long as it requires to get the information we need. We must search the archives of all the knowledge we have acquired during the past ten thousand years and try to find the key to blend our life forms into one. In the meantime, I suggest you return to the Old Ones, find out how many are willing to transfer their spirits in this way and have them report to Xanthu's clinic to have their profiles recorded. I wish I could tell you more but I cannot at this time."

Quetzie rose and smoothed her robe. "There are also things I wish I could tell you," she said. "This is the time because you have done everything I asked you to do. . . but I do not have the words, and I cannot open my mind to you because this is something that goes deeper than the mind. Can you possibly understand?"

"No, Quetzie, we cannot understand," Xanthu said. "That is not as important as you think. Tsunor and I once reached a high level of spiritual evolution. Something went wrong and we find we yet have much to learn. It will require hundreds, perhaps thousands of additional lives on this planet before we even begin to understand ourselves. As regards the ultimate understanding, we are all still children."

"You're still treating me like a child!" Quetzie said. and stamped her foot. "You tell me I'm as old as you are and then you act superior because you remember it and I don't." She swept her dark eyes over the three faces smiling up at her, clenched her fists, then collapsed on the floor with them again, laughing. "Oh, I love you so much!"

"That's where we began and that's where we're going," Xanthu said. "I hope."

The weeks which followed were filled with dedicated work, laughter and nightmare. Albar stood mute with amazement when he learned the infinitesimal detail with which Tsunor planned to examine his physical body but underwent the ordeal with only whimsical indignation. Quetzie often emerged dull-eyed and spent from her long hours in immobile levitation while Tsunor probed delicately into her body, seeking to modify the girl's organic structure and genetic alignment to assure physical survival for the unborn child. Xanthu, when he learned the child was to be male, narrowed his studies of the Old Ones' profiles to the men, believing that even a slightly mutated life form should not have the initial disadvantage of beginning a new earth life in an unfamiliar sex.

When Xanthu was ready to personally interview the males of the Old Ones. . . they had unanimously elected to become spirit donors. . . the first applicant to appear in his clinic was his own father. Startled, he was belated in the traditional greeting of lowering his head and sending a telepathic wish for love and continued spiritual growth. "Father! I did not expect you. . ."

The older man was a few inches shorter than his son and somewhat thicker. Otherwise, they were similiar in appearance except for the older man's eyes, which were sunken and slightly luminescent. He smiled, amused. "I did not ask to be first, Xanthu, so I cannot tell you if this honor is due to my age or your position."

"But father, you are not that. . . old?" Xanthu caught the good humor in his father's mind and they chuckled together.

"I am somewhere between three and four hundred years old. The exact number is no longer important. I am here to answer the questions you will ask. Please proceed."

Xanthu remained silent, letting his mind run back thousands of years to a time when he and his father had been friends but not related. Like the man facing him, now his father, Xanthu had been one of the first to assume physical form on earth, bringing with him his own specialized knowledge. His father, then as now, was a hortoculturist, breeding, developing and growing nourishing plant life. At the time when Xanthu and most of his kind had forsaken spiritual development for the pleasures available through virtually unlimited power on a new planet, the man who was now his father had returned to spirit in futility and disgust. That the older man had chosen a new life on this freshly-born and savage continent was due to his higher spiritual evolvement, not guilt as was the case with Xanthu and Tsunor.

The father, participating in these thoughts, broke them by speaking aloud. "The Infinite has left many doors through which we may go forward," he said. "I want to take part in what you are doing because it is new and exciting. If I am not eligible for this, I will bring myself to earth again in human form at some future date. The potential complexities of this race will offer unlimited challenges. Even if I accomplish little, I feel I will enjoy the experiences."

"But you won't be able to retain your skills," Xanthu said. "Not without the Memory."

"I will retain some recall of them. Besides, I am wondering if our precious Memory is really serving these people. I, for one, am useless. I have cultures in my laboratory which I could germinate within days and seed the earth to the horizon. But the earth is covered with the jungle. Nothing available in the Memory has enabled us to conquer it. I think the Ayas will conquer it, though, and I want to be on hand as one of them."

"I wish I could share your optimism, father. It's practically a mathematical certainty. The jungle will win."

"There are more hospitable lands to the North."

"Agreed. And how shall we reach them. . . through the jungle?

Or hack through to the coast and ask these people to build sea-going ships, people who have never seen the ocean? They have only heard of the sea in tales passed down by their forebearers".

"It is being done by those on the other continent they call Atlantis," the father said. "That land is developing according to a somewhat different pattern."

"I know little of it," Xanthu said absently. "I was taken there astrally while in training but that was over a hundred years ago. You apparently know much more of the world than I."

The older man shrugged. "What else is there for a weary mind which needs no sleep? I do not go there often for it depresses me. Those of our kind are losing their ascendency with a fast-growing population. There are evil factions, and factions within factions."

"I wish at least we knew the secret of their population growth," Xanthu said.

The older man widened his eyes, surprised. "That's no secret. Many from our own Muror are again bringing their spirits to earth in purely human form, and retaining much of the Memory."

Xanthu smiled ruefully. "That is a hazard of being over-trained. One loses touch with other fields. How do they do it, bring the Memory to incarnate form?"

"Different evolutionary pattern as I said," his father said. "We can't do it with our own people unless, of course, this experiment of yours is successful. Do you think it will be?"

"The transference is possible. I have determined that. Physiologically there are still many imponderables which only Tsunor knows. I will not be able to talk with her until our next rest-time." Xanthu smiled. "But we are here met to determine YOUR suitability, are we not?"

"My profile is in the minds of your assistants," the other man said without changing expression. "They are in the next room awaiting your call."

Xanthu half-closed his eyes for a few seconds, then looked directly into his father's face. "Your profile is not consistent with the pattern we are seeking to establish for this initial birth."

"That is disappointing but not surprising. Will you continue the experiments, even if this one is a failure?"

"We have little choice," Xanthu said. "Quetzie has vowed to continue getting pregnant. . . if she survives."

"So it is that critical, is it?" The man rose to go. "I will seal myself in my cubicle and send my spirit to aid you."

"Thank you, father. That is generous."

And a child was born. Quetzie scorned anesthesia and levitation and sent Albar to the ranks of the workers for a midwife. Xanthu and Tsunor attended the birth but took no part until it was over and Tsunor, with courtesy and deference, showed the awed midwife how to stem the blood flow with fingertip pressure in the abdominal area. The secrecy of Quetzie's confinement had been absolute, known only to the Rulers and to Albar. They could not, in keeping with their code, restrain the midwife or block the events from her mind without her consent. A cursory probing of her mind revealed that she was incapable of grasping the impact of what had happened. They shrugged to each other and sent the woman back to her people as the harbinger of the most momentous news of her generation.

The Council convened when the child was six weeks old and it had been found healthy by Tsunor, and Xanthu had satisfied himself that the ancient spirit in truth lived in the new body. The thirteen-member Council had not met in formal session for nearly forty years; all were assigned other duties and their highly refined telepathy enabled them to blend their consciousnesses within seconds when the occasion demanded. It was known only to the Rulers themselves who comprised the Council. Albar, nonplussed, looked from face to face, recognizing one of his teachers and others he had known all his life but had never suspected were members of the august Council.

Ill at ease, Albar sat between Xanthu and Tsunor, facing the Council who sat comfortably on their pads on the floor across the narrow room. Quetzie was absent although her mind was tuned to the proceedings. Hoping to ease Albar's tenseness, Xanthu linked their minds and twitted Quetzie on her uncharacteristic solemnity and decorum. The thought bounced back that she was on her way to let the baby soil Xanthu's bed.

The Council Spokesman made a soft request for attention. "We have a situation thrust upon us which could alter the future of the race on this continent," he said. "There are those of us who think it is long overdue. Others question the methods by which it was accomplished. We are unanimous, however, in agreeing that the ultimate choice was in no way in our hands. An exceptionally strong-willed member of our community has imposed her actions on us in a manner which we, as a collective body, had neither the courage nor imagination to undertake." The Spokesman paused and Quetzie's subdued little-girl giggle ran through all minds. Several of the Council lowered their heads to hide smiles.

"The question is now, where do we go from this point." The Spokesman turned to Albar. "Albar, since we technically exist only to serve you and your people, you are the highest ranking member of this assemblage and thus have the right of first expression."

Albar drew his feet under him and looked into the faces of the Council. "The subtleties of beginning the mixed mating between your women and us are beyond me," he said slowly. "I can only present certain ideas Quetzie and I have discussed and request to proceed with them." Sensing the complete sympathy he was being accorded, he gained confidence. "If we are to begin the new race, or life form if you prefer, we think it would be better to do so in the surroundings and under the same difficulties in which our people now live."

"Then you are suggesting that you and Quetzie take your child to live with your people," the Spokesman said

"That is correct."

"But you are temple trained, Albar. You have no skills to offer to help retain a hold on the precious area we have only barely subdued in over five hundred years."

"I have thought of that," Albar said. "It is because I have spent my life in the temple that I have much to offer. Surely you have not kept us in the temple all these years as servants. We have enjoyed, we realize, separate but equal privileges."

"No," the Spokesman said. "We have attempted to develop the intellectual strain as we found it. You have been taught all this."

"Then it is time to put it to use," Albar said. "We have no written language from which to learn of our past failures and few successes. You have not needed it. . . and we have not needed it because you were always at hand with whatever information we required. But it is now fairly obvious that you cannot survive. It is possible that we can. I propose to devise a language and teach it to the children too young to work."

Xanthu spoke. "With the Council's permission. . . the mated couple of Elan and Trona were adepts at linguistics in Muror before our telepathy was developed. My father tells me the priesthood in Atlantis uses written language symbols. Their heirarchy differs from ours but I am sure they would cooperate. I can work out the details of transmission if there is some manner of sending Elan and Trona there in either spirit or body. Is this possible?"

The Council combined their minds for a half minute. A woman in the white robe of a ceremonial priestess said, "It is theoretically possible, although it has not been attempted since the destruction of the original continent of Muror and the alteration of the earth's magnetic field. Would Elan and Trona be willing to accept this mission?"

"They can be called," Xanthu said. "This is their rest-time." He sent the call, which was answered immediately and in the affirmative.

"We are progressing further than I had hoped," the Spokesman said. "Let us now hear from Tsunor. Have you spoken with all our women who are of child-bearing capabilities?"

"Yes," Tsunor said. "They number a hundred and two. All are willing to bear children although several are hesitant to leave the temple to mingle with the workers." She smiled and pressed Albar's hand. "They fear they will not be accepted by your people, especially your women. It is evident from many experiences that WE women find you men attractive," she added with quiet, amused irony.

Quetzie broke in. "Then direct them to attend the great festival you have authorized to celebrate the birth of our child. They will learn the simple beauty of these people at first hand, they will love them as I do, and from love can come children. I think I have demonstrated this satisfactorily."

"Um, yes," the Spokesman said. "We were hoping for a more dignified and orderly merging of our forces."

"There is nothing more dignified than a pregnant woman trying to walk without wobbling," Quetzie said.

"Yes. We will go into that later," the Spokesman said. "If there are no other thoughts we will adjourn to our respective duties." They stood and the woman in the white robe said, "Xanthu, will you call Elan and Trona so the four of us can meet this afternoon in your clinic? I have nothing more for now." All made the ceremonial salute to each other and filed out of the room.

Xanthu held Albar's arm as they followed the Council. "I would like for you to attend this meeting with us," he said. "I'm sure you will find it most interesting."

"I promise not to bring Quetzie," Albar said as they parted.

The priestess arrived early, inspired by Xanthu's invitation to sample Albar's witch's brew coffee. Albar was brewing a second pot when Elan and Trona arrived, precisely on time, holding hands. They were called the twins because they refused to be separated and had the charming habit of flashing their thoughts to each other and frequently speaking in unison, both aloud and telepathically. When only one spoke it was usually Trona, the woman, while her mate scanned the minds of those they were talking to in order to have an instantaneous reply ready. They were stimulating but occasionally exhausting conversationalists. They worked tirelessly at refining and simplifying the spoken language into a musical poetry of sound. They sampled the coffee, pronounced it good, then spoke in unison to the priestess, "Have you found a way to transport us to Atlantis?"

"Several possibilities present themselves," the priestess said. "The most ideal would be if we could build a flying machine but, although we have the knowledge, we do not have the equipment. We could project you there astrally but it would take a good deal of training and practice to be able to remain for a significant length of time. Another choice would be to suspend your bodies and project your consciousness in fairly substantial physical form. I object to this because your suspended bodies could deteriorate. The most logical way would be teleportation of your present selves, intact. How are you at levitation?"

"Sadly out of practice," Elan and Trona said. "We have not used it for fifty years. We found it tends to soften the muscle tone."

"That could be re-learned," the priestess said. "The projection itself poses the biggest problem. It would require the combined efforts of at least fifty of us, working in an unfamiliar magnetic field. It would have to be done in stages, like the surges of electrical impulses. You would have to remain in levitation for perhaps several days because you would be materializing frequently over open water. It would require quite a bit of training and practice."
"How much training?" Albar said. "And for how long?"

"Thirty years. Twenty under ideal conditions."

Albar heaved a monstrous sign. "I have already lived thirty years. In another thirty I will be an old man, nearing the end of productivity."

The priestess was instantly contrite. "I'm sorry, Albar. I was so enmeshed in technicalities that I lost sight of the fact that we are making the entire effort for your benefit."

"For the benefit of us all," Albar said. "The planning of future history can never be the work of one person."

"We are still working in the realm of theory," Xanthu said. "We have by no means exhausted the possibilities."

"We have a thought," Trona said. "All earth languages are in some way similar because they came from the memory of past lives. However, they evolve independently according to local need. We have seen, and been partly responsible for, a definite linguistic shift during the three generations we have worked with these people in this area." Without pause, Elan joined his mate and they completed the conversation together. "If we are to begin the building of a new race, why not construct our own language?"

"Where do we begin?" Xanthu said. He held up his hands. "I have used written language on other planets many hundreds of thousands of years ago. . . but not with appendages such as this nor did I inhabit a body in any way similar to this one."

"There are those among my people who can write," Albar said, excited. "The descendents of the artisans who decorated the original temples and public buildings in the city. The skills have been preserved with each generation. Surely you have noticed the ornate designs on many houses. . . and even the patterns dyed into the clothes we wear!"

"Get them!" Elan and Trona said, pulling Albar to his feet and wrapping their arms around him. "We will isolate individual phonetic sounds and your artists shall design symbols for them. Come!" At the doorway they stopped and whirled, almost jerking Albar off his feet. "May we have Council's permission?" The priestess, laughing, waved them from the room.

Firmly but with love, the Council restrained Quetzie's impulsiveness and undertook the profiling of male Ayas between the ages of twenty and thirty. Only the unmated males were considered and the screening was so rigorous that only four hundred applicants were considered acceptable. Even so, there was a loud outcry from the female workers which was quieted only when the Council, with grave misgivings, consented to polygamous matings upon consent of all participating parties.

The altering of the bodies of the fertile women was made easier for Tsunor due to what she had learned with her initial experiences with Quetzie and the fact that the none of them were at the time pregnant. Despite this, some two dozen of them found the modifications too arduous and were granted Return Transition after taking a solemn vow to return their spirits to the newborn resulting from liasons between Ruler women and worker men.

— ⊃ ⊂ —

A segment of the population surrounding the central temple was removed to unoccupied homes further away and the new community began to grow. To accustom the divergent life forms to each other and affect a harmony of living through habit, contraception was enforced during the first five years. This rule was excepted for Albar and Quetzie who, however, did not reside in what soon became known as the "temple commune" but lived apart in a distant sector of the city with Elan and Trona, embarked on a lifetime project of developing a written language and training future teachers. Albar and Quetzie found time to produce a child every fourteen months with mathematical regularity. Requests for the Return Transition from the Old Ones stopped; they awaited their opportunities as spirit donors with gracious patience.

There were failures as spirit donors miscalculated the moment of transference and children were born uninhabited, and died. Strict birth control was regretfully established when it was learned that the Ruler women could reproduce only in conjunction with a Ruler spirit donor. The new population had reached a stasis several years before Albar became a grandfather. Albar's grandchild was watched carefully, as were two subsequent births within the family. Satisfied, the Council met formally for the last time at the end of twenty-five years.

"We will not meet again," the Spokesman said with characteristic lack of preliminaries. "The second generation of our racial blending has begun. We cannot predict either success or failure. We hope for ultimate success, of course. In any event, we no longer serve a useful function, and I hereby declare this Council dissolved as of the termination of this sitting. At this time we direct certain essential personnel such as metal refiners, tool makers, teachers and a few others to remain on this plane for a period of one hundred years. At the end of this time they may offer themselves as spirit donors or make the option of the Return Transition by means which will be left available to them. The remainder of us, some five hundred in number, are at liberty to opt for Return Transition or as additional spirit donors, for which there is still a great demand. The last residents on this planet of our kind will be those who have conceived and borne children. They may remain as they desire, although few have voiced that desire knowing they can no longer bear children when no further spirit donors are available. Disseminate these instructions as soon as is practical. We are adjourned."

The pioneering attitude of the spirit donors was infectious and when the decisions of the Council were made public fewer than a hundred of the remaining Ruler population chose the Return Transition. These, for reasons of their own, were impatient and Xanthu spent an exhausting year and a half harmonizing the consciousnesses of these beings, easing them over to their original existence and vaporizing the bodies by converting them into energy in the form of a momentary blinding light which dissipated itself in seconds. Without the familiar guidance of the Council, the remaining spirit donors were restless unless assigned make-work tasks while awaiting their turn to enter the body of an infant. Over thirty years elapsed before the final donor, the Council Spokesman, breathed a relieved sign as he released his life force from his five hundred year old body into that of a brown-skinned baby.

Infinitely weary and lonely with the first idleness they had known on this planet, Xanthu and Tsunor walked the streets to Albar's academy which had grown to a dozen buildings. They sought out Quetzie but declined her offer of a guided tour of the institution. "It's just as well," she said, leading them to the rooftop of the building in which they lived. "I know very little about either the function or organization of this place. Elan and Trona are the life forces here. And Albar."

"Oh?" Tsunor said. "Is Albar still active?"

Quetzie laughed in pure delight, shaking her head until static crackled from her hair as it swung around her shoulders. "Active is the word for it. He mated with one of his students when he was past sixty, has had two more children with a third on the way." She stopped and looked at Tsunor, her eyes dancing. "Oh, Tsunor, don't look so prim. Having neither the Memory nor a soul mate, I feel quite mortal and human. . . and contented with this life style."

"What are your plans now, Quetzie?" Xanthu said.

"You mean, now that I can have no more children?" She became serious. "I was more fortunate than most, being able to bear ten children before I was sterilized. . . and those ten have given me forty or fifty grand and great-grandchildren." She paused and looked over the city which was nearly silent during the midday rest time. "I think I shall become a goddess."

"A goddess!" Xanthu and Tsunor spoke together, startled.

"A high priestess, at least," she said, disarming them with the pixie smile that had remained undimmed for over fifty years. "I think I have a certain advantage by never having attained the Memory. I remember only this life, on earth, and feel no pull toward other lives, other realms of existence. I do have longevity to look forward to in the only world I know so I intend to use it."

"But what is this priestess business?" Xanthu said.

"See here, Xanthu, you have always taught that the Universe is founded on love and spirituality. But I have only your word for that. I have never experienced it. However, I do believe it so in order to experience it I feel I must create it, work myself into it. . . and lead my people with me as I learn."

"But Quetzie, you don't know the rituals, and all who would teach you are now gone. You are welcome to use the temple, of course. . ."

"I'm making up my own rituals as I go along. Now, that isn't as haphazard as it sounds. Like you, I seldom sleep. Once a week I meditate throughout the night and then hold a sunrise service for whomever wants to attend. Right now it's mostly the older students. Being telepathic, I'm receptive to their reactions. When it's good, I keep the ritual and polish it. If it's not so good, I discard it. I had planned to use the temple but not until I've trained myself more, another twenty years or so."

"I can find no fault with that," Xanthu said. Tsunor nodded agreement. "We owe you so much," he went on. "The people owe you more. It has been more dramatically successful than I suppose even you imagined."

"No," she said. "I visualized this, and also what it can be in three or four centuries." She flashed an impish grin. "After all, I intend to be around to supervise."

Xanthu was silent, half hearing the city as it awoke to begin its afternoon tasks. "Does all this have to do with your absolute fanaticism at the beginning? You were unable to explain it to us at the time."

"Yes," she said quietly. "It has everything to do with it. A leader is coming to guide this people, a Great One. I do not know how this came to me but this man could only be born as a product of the melding of our two life forms. He will be one of my direct descendents, although I have no idea if I will still be on the earth at that time. It is from him that I took my name. His name will be Quetzecoatl."

"It sounds like a beautiful life, Quetzie," Tsunor said, her voice deep with emotion.

"Won't you stay and share it with me?"

"You do us great honor, dear friend, but Xanthu and I are very tired. We have a great longing for another planet which we have not visited since before this earth was formed. We will rest there. In a few hundred years we will return and seek you out. Goodbye, Quetzie." They held each other in a long embrace, kissed each other, then walked down from the rooftop to the street, turning to wave as they began their final long walk to the temple.

Keeping a stately, cadenced stride they made a leisurly tour of the temple, the great hall built to accommodate thousands, the cool thick walled corridors, the learning rooms and workshops, deserted now except for an occasional solitary Ruler who worked out his final allotted task with calm purpose and who smiled them a brief greeting, then a fonder farewell when he realized their destination. They went lastly to Xanthu's clinic and greeted the attendant on duty. "Will you go now, Xanthu?" the attendant said.

"Later, just before dawn," Xanthu said. "The equipment is set for automatic operation. You need not stay." They went to their rooms and when the heat of the day had passed, to their rooftop. They thrilled as the heavens darkened and the stars appeared, intensely aware of the infinite Universe and the power which would soon sweep them undreamed-of distances through it.

"Have we done well, or have we failed?" Tsunor said, her face nestled warmly into his throat.

"I do not know if we have done well, Tsunor. That will be judged by those who remain here, the future generations. Failed? Oh, no. We have known much love in this place, and one can never equate love with failure."

They held each other through the hours of the night, not speaking, serene and contented. They knew when the time arrived. Arms tightly around each other's waists, they descended quietly and purposefully to the clinic. They lay together on the pallet Xanthu had built to accommodate them both. As Xanthu activated the switch they joined their last moment of earthly consciousness in a vast surge of love over the stilled city. Few remembered it upon awakening but at that moment thousands stirred in their sleep.

And awoke refreshed.

We have enjoyed noting our personal reactions to our varied past lives as they unfolded. Most evoked a certain nostalgia, sometimes tinged with sadness, but we responded to who we were and who we knew during those times with love. The far-out span known by Xanthu and Tsunor, however, left us with a feeling of near awe, more exhaustion than exhilaration. The clarity of memory which expands through immeasurable reaches of time and space is numbing when we try to compute it in terms of mortal reckoning. The incredible vista down the nearly timeless corridor connecting us to a younger, emerging world tunes the spiritual ear again to the haunting echoes of thunder.

We could not recognize ourselves in the bodies we then inhabited; the very land masses were totally unfamiliar. It is not unreasonable to wonder if the planet itself circled the sun in a different orbit, perhaps with 30-hour days and an entirely altered global climate. We are all individual segments in space without limit and time which cannot be measured. How then can we comprehend the endlessness of eternity when we have trouble visualizing our own earth during another phase of being, with other civilizations flourishing for millennia and passing into oblivion without a trace--except for the tenuous recollections of a few newly-opened minds like ours?

But how long ago, in terms we can understand? Keetoowah says it was five hundred million years ago, give or take a few shifts of the polar axis. He was there, too, as my father again. (He mentioned once that he feels an occasional impulse to call me "son" but is put off when he looks at my gray beard.) That's a lot of years but not an unreasonable number. Even the most pragmatic scientist will support the thesis that our world has been here considerably longer than that. I can neither verify nor dispute Keetoowah's numbering system but, lacking other evidence, I'm inclined to accept it. He's been right on target with dozens of other happenings which I can support with my own memory patterns. He arrived at that half-billion figure intuitively, the same intuition which almost makes me dizzy as I grasp at fragments of a Cosmos so vast that man can not even imagine it.

Just because specific memories elude me, such as the chronological setting of this final story, doesn't mean events didn't take place. I reject the word, "impossible". It only has meaning within our own experiences. Any patient scientist, for example, can demonstrate the validity of gravitation to me, how it is "impossible" for a solid body of matter to rise unaided from the earth's surface, and why any loosened object must inevitably roll downhill. Yet within my experience are events reversing this so-called law. I have seen, and experienced, levitation. It happened to me only twice, but should I deny my own senses and the senses of those who witnessed it because scientific fact says it's "impossible"? There are a number of places throughout the United States where an object as heavy as an automobile will roll uphill if left out of gear with the brakes off. Surveyors' instruments have ruled out optical illusion. This has been verified by thousands, yet a sober study of Newtonian physics will prove it is all "impossible".

Very little needs to be added to the story to establish a relationship of who we were then. . . and are now. We were discovering our mistakes and trying to correct them, then as now. The story of Xanthu and Tsunor ended indecisively but on a hopeful note. Our own story will end in a few years and we certainly don't know precisely what will happen then, but we're unafraid and quite hopeful. We feel that any life during which truth is learned is a good life.